Massachusetts

THE THIRTEEN COLONIES

Massachusetts

CRAIG A. DOHERTY

KATHERINE M. DOHERTY

Facts On File, Inc.

Note on Photos: Many of the illustrations and photographs used in this book are old, historical images. The quality of the prints is not always up to current standards, as in some cases the originals are from old or poor-quality negatives or are damaged. The content of the illustrations, however, made their inclusion important despite problems in reproduction.

Massachusetts

Facts On File, Inc.
132 West 31st Street
New York NY 10001

Library of Congress Cataloging-in-Publication
Doherty, Craig A.
    Massachusetts / Craig A. Doherty and Katherine M. Doherty.
        p. cm. — (The thirteen colonies)
    Includes bibliographical references (p.) and index.
    ISBN 0-8160-5407-X (acid-free paper)
    1. Massachusetts—History—Colonial period, ca. 1600–1775—Juvenile
    literature. 2. Massachusetts—History—1775–1865—Juvenile literature.
    [1. Massachusetts—History—Colonial period, ca. 1600–1775.
    2. Massachusetts—History—1775–1865.] I. Doherty, Katherine M. II. Title.
    F67.D64 2005
    974.4'02—dc22   2003024289

Facts On File books are available at special discounts when purchased in bulk quantities for businesses, associations, institutions, or sales promotions. Please call our Special Sales Department in New York at (212) 967-8800 or (800) 322-8755.

You can find Facts On File on the World Wide Web at http://www.factsonfile.com

Text design by Erika K. Arroyo
Cover design by Semadar Megged
Maps and graph by Dale Williams

Printed in the United States of America

VB FOF 10 9 8 7 6 5 4 3 2 1

This book is printed on acid-free paper.

Contents

Introduction

In the 11th century, Vikings from Scandinavia sailed to North America. They explored the Atlantic coast and set up a few small settlements. In Newfoundland and Nova Scotia, Canada, archaeologists have found traces of these settlements. No one knows for sure why they did not establish permanent colonies. It may have been that it was too far away from their homeland. At about the same time, many Scandinavians were involved with raiding and establishing settlements along the coasts of what are now Great Britain and France. This may have offered greater rewards than traveling all the way to North America.

When the western part of the Roman Empire fell in 476, Europe lapsed into a period of almost 1,000 years of war, plague, and hardship. This period of European history is often referred to as the Dark Ages or Middle Ages. Communication between the different parts of Europe was almost nonexistent. If other Europeans knew about the Vikings' explorations westward, they left no record of it. Between the time of Viking exploration and Christopher Columbus's 1492 journey, Europe underwent many changes.

By the 15th century, Europe had experienced many advances. Trade within the area and with the Far East had created prosperity for the governments and many wealthy people. The Catholic Church had become a rich and powerful institution. Although wars would be fought and governments would come and go, the countries of Western Europe had become fairly strong. During this time, Europe rediscovered many of the arts and sciences that had

Vikings explored the Atlantic coast of North America in ships similar to this one. *(National Archives of Canada)*

existed before the fall of Rome. They also learned much from their trade with the Near and Far East. Historians refer to this time as the Renaissance, which means "rebirth."

At this time, some members of the Catholic Church did not like the direction the church was going. People such as Martin Luther and John Calvin spoke out against the church. They soon gained a number of followers who decided that they would protest and form their own churches. The members of these new churches were called Protestants. The movement to establish these new churches is called the Protestant Reformation. It would have a big impact on America as many Protestant groups would leave Europe so they could worship the way they wanted to.

In addition to religious dissent, problems arose with the overland trade routes to the Far East. The Ottoman Turks took control of the lands in the Middle East and disrupted trade. It was at this time that European explorers began trying to find a water route to the Far East. The explorers first sailed around Africa. Then an Italian named Christopher Columbus convinced the king and queen of Spain that it would be shorter to sail west to Asia rather than go around Africa. Most sailors and educated people at the time knew the world was round. However, Columbus made two errors in his calculations. First, he did not realize just how big the Earth is, and second, he did not know that the continents of North and South America blocked a westward route to Asia.

When Columbus made landfall in 1492, he believed that he was in the Indies, as the Far East was called at the time. For a period of time after Columbus, the Spanish controlled the seas and the exploration of what was called the New World. England tried to compete with the Spanish on the high seas, but their ships were no match for the floating fortresses of the Spanish Armada. These heavy ships, known as galleons, ruled the Atlantic.

In 1588, that all changed. A fleet of English ships fought a series of battles in which their smaller but faster and more maneuverable ships finally defeated the Spanish Armada. This opened up the New World to anyone willing to cross the ocean. Portugal, Holland, France, and England all funded voyages of exploration to the New World. In North America, the French explored the far north. The Spanish had already established colonies in what are now Florida, most of the Caribbean, and much of Central and South America. The Dutch

Depicted in this painting, Christopher Columbus completed three additional voyages to the Americas after his initial trip in search of a westward route to Asia in 1492. *(Library of Congress, Prints and Photographs Division [LC-USZ62-103980])*

bought Manhattan and would establish what would become New York, as well as various islands in the Caribbean and lands in South America. The English claimed most of the east coast of North America and set about creating colonies in a variety of ways.

Companies were formed in England and given royal charters to set up colonies. Some of the companies sent out military and trade expeditions to find gold and other riches. They employed men such as John Smith, Bartholomew Gosnold, and others to explore the lands they had been granted. Other companies found groups of Protestants who wanted to leave England and worked out deals that let them establish colonies. No matter what circumstances a colony was established under, the first settlers suffered hardships as

After Columbus's exploration of the Americas, the Spanish controlled the seas, largely because of their galleons, or large, heavy ships, that looked much like this model. *(Library of Congress, Prints and Photographs Division, [LC-USZ62-103297])*

they tried to build communities in what to them was a wilderness. They also had to deal with the people who were already there.

Native Americans lived in every corner of the Americas. There were vast and complex civilizations in Central and South America. The city that is now known as Cahokia was located along the Mississippi River in what is today Illinois and may have had as many as 50,000 residents. The people of Cahokia built huge earthen mounds that can still be seen today. There has been a lot of speculation as to the total population of Native Americans in 1492. Some have put the number as high as 40 million people.

Most of the early explorers encountered Native Americans. They often wrote descriptions of them for the people of Europe. They also kidnapped a few of these people, took them back to Europe, and put them on display. Despite the number of Native Americans, the Europeans still claimed the land as their own. The rulers of Europe and the Catholic Church at the time felt they had a right to take any lands they wanted from people who did not share their level of technology and who were not Christians.

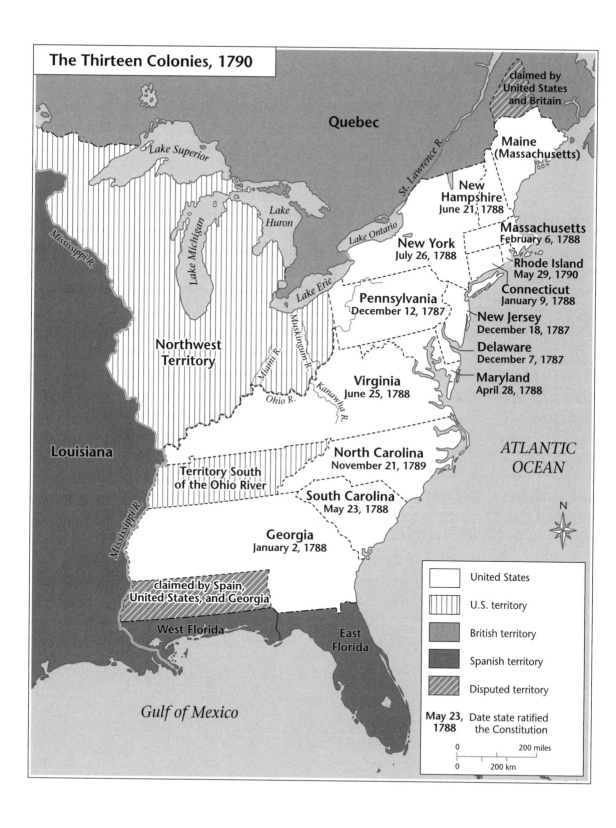

The Thirteen Colonies, 1790

Quebec

Lake Superior

Lake Michigan

Lake Huron

Lake Erie

Lake Ontario

Mississippi R.

St. Lawrence R.

claimed by United States and Britain

Maine (Massachusetts)

New Hampshire
June 21, 1788

Massachusetts
February 6, 1788

New York
July 26, 1788

Rhode Island
May 29, 1790

Connecticut
January 9, 1788

Pennsylvania
December 12, 1787

New Jersey
December 18, 1787

Delaware
December 7, 1787

Maryland
April 28, 1788

Northwest Territory

Muskingum R.

Miami R.

Ohio R.

Kanawha R.

Virginia
June 25, 1788

Louisiana

Territory South
of the Ohio River

North Carolina
November 21, 1789

South Carolina
May 23, 1788

ATLANTIC OCEAN

N

Georgia
January 2, 1788

Mississippi R.

claimed by Spain,
United States, and Georgia

West Florida

East Florida

Gulf of Mexico

United States

U.S. territory

British territory

Spanish territory

Disputed territory

May 23, 1788   Date state ratified
                the Constitution

0   200 miles
0   200 km

1

First Contacts

A number of explorers had visited the Atlantic coast of North America during the 16th century. Then in 1602, Bartholomew Gosnold explored much of the New England coast. On this voyage, he sailed near Cape Cod and named it for the abundance of codfish that were in the waters off the cape. Gosnold also kidnapped a few Native Americans to take back to England. In 1614, John Smith, who also led settlers to Virginia, sailed along the Massachusetts coast. Smith wrote about his explorations in a book titled *A Description of New England*. The descriptions of New England in Smith's book caused many to think about leaving England for the New World.

Thanks to these voyages and others, England established its claim to the coast from Maine to Florida. During this time, fishermen from Europe came and set up temporary settlements along the coast so they could dry cod and the other fish they caught. The entire coast was already populated by numerous Native American tribes. These Native Americans were descended from Paleo-Indians who arrived in the area 10,000 year ago at the end of the last ice age.

In what was to become the colony of Massachusetts, there were a number of different tribes. Anthropologists call these Native Americans Eastern Woodland Indians, which refers to their culture. Eastern Woodland Indians are often considered in two groups: Northeast and Southeast. Native Americans are also grouped by the languages they spoke. All of the various tribes in the area of

1

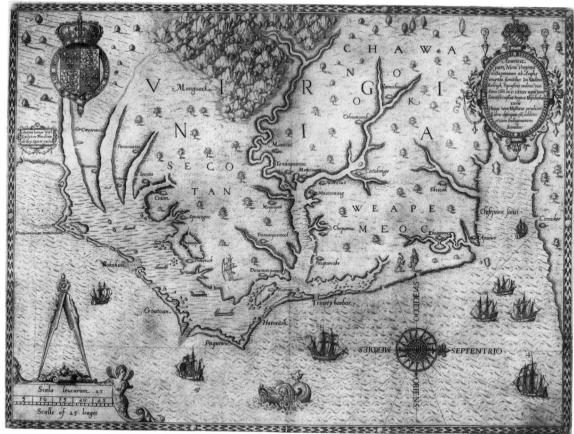

John Smith's descriptions of the colonies generated much interest in them. This particular map of Virginia was published in one of Smith's books about his explorations. *(Library of Congress, Prints and Photographs Division [LC-USZ62-116706])*

present-day Massachusetts spoke some form of Algonquian language. The tribes of the area each had their own name and territory.

The colony took its name from the Massachuset tribe that lived in the area that is now metropolitan Boston. Some believe that there may have been as many as 3,000 members of the Massachuset tribe at the beginning of the 17th century. They lived in 20 separate villages. Some of the tribes that lived in the area surrounding the Massachuset were the Wampanoag, Pawtuxet, Nauset, Penacook, Nipmuc, and Narragansett tribes. They all spoke a similar Algonquian dialect and communicated with each other regularly.

All these tribes lived similar lives. Their primary subsistence came from farming. Corn, beans, and squash were their staples.

Description of New England

Captain John Smith wrote a lot about his voyages in hopes of promoting interest in the colonies. The following is part of the description of New England from his *Advertisements for the Inexperienced Planters of New England*, published in London in 1631.

This Country we now speak of lieth betwixt 41° and 44 1/2°, the very mean for heat and cold betwixt the Equinoctial and the North Pole, in which I have sounded about five and twenty very good harbors; in many whereof is anchorage for five hundred good ships of any burden, in some of them for a thousand: and more than three hundred isles overgrown with good timber or divers sorts of other woods; in most of them (in their seasons) plenty of wild fruits, fish, and fowl, and pure springs of most excellent water pleasantly distilling from their rocky foundations.

When the English discovered the abundance of Atlantic cod along the coast of the New World, many of them set up temporary settlements in which they could dry the fish to transport and then sell it. Detail of a 1715 map by Herman Moll, this illustration shows the process off the coast of Newfoundland. *(Library of Congress)*

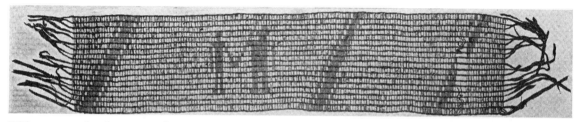

With uses ranging from recording agreements to sending messages, wampum became more important in trade for tribes in the Massachusetts area after the arrival of European explorers and settlers. *(Library of Congress, Prints and Photographs Division [LC-USZ62-86486])*

They also grew tobacco, which was used in many of their ceremonies. In addition to farming, they caught fish and harvested large quantities of shellfish. They used the shells of clams to make into strands called wampum. They used wampum to trade with each other and as jewelry. In addition to fishing and farming, they supplemented their diets by hunting.

Their villages were located near their fields, which they usually cleared by burning. When the soil in an area would start to yield less, they would create new fields by burning more forest. Their homes were called longhouses and often housed the members of one extended family. A longhouse was made of a frame of posts and poles and then covered with bark. Fires in the center of the

To protect themselves, some tribes of the Northeast culture area to which the Massachuset belong built stockades, or a perimeter, around their villages made of tall timbers, sharpened at one end and driven into the ground. *(Library of Congress)*

longhouse were used for cooking and heat in the winter. In the summer months, the cooking fires would be outside.

The explorers and fishermen who visited the area before permanent non-Indian settlers arrived in 1620 brought death and destruction to the Massachuset and other tribes of New England. Between 1614 and 1617, 75 percent of the Massachuset tribe died of European diseases. The Native Americans had no immunity to common European diseases. Of the estimated 3,000 Massachuset Indians in 1600, only 750 were left in 1620.

THE PILGRIMS

Henry VIII, king of England, had a number of differences with the Catholic Church. Between 1529 and 1536, he caused Parliament to enact a number of laws that separated the church in England from Rome. This created the Church of England, also called the Anglican Church. Although no longer under the control of the pope in Rome, the Church of England did not tolerate dissent from its official doctrines. To disagree with England's church was considered treason and could be punished with imprisonment or even death.

Despite the possible penalties, there were people who did not agree with the way the Church of England forced them to worship. Some of these people left the Church of England to form their own churches. They were often referred to as Separatists. One such group was organized in the small village of Scrooby in Nottinghamshire in 1606. Their leaders included William Brewster, Richard Clifton, and William Bradford. Once the group was established, it was forced to move from England to avoid persecution. Bradford later became the second governor of Plymouth Colony, a post he would hold for more than 30 years.

They first went to the English town of Boston where the group's leaders were put in prison. Once released, they moved again,

William Brewster led a group of Pilgrims known as the Separatists, who left the Church of England to form their own church and settled in North America to avoid persecution. *(Library of Congress, Prints and Photographs Division [LC-USZ62-12707])*

finally deciding to leave England for Holland in 1609. In Holland, people were allowed the freedom to worship as they saw fit. The group from Scrooby settled in the Dutch city of Leiden and was free to conduct their religious practices.

Although the Dutch did not interfere with their religion, the English were foreigners living in exile. They found it hard to live and prosper. They were also proud of their English heritage and did not want their children to lose that. In 1618 the group decided to move one more time. If they returned to England, they would end up back in jail or worse. It seemed the only place they could go was to the New World.

The group's records show that they talked about going to South America but were concerned about the climate and the Spanish. They were also afraid that if they went to the new English colony of Virginia, they would face the same religious persecution that awaited them in England. Other ideas were suggested and rejected until the group felt their only choice was to go to Virginia and set up their own colony far away from where people had already settled.

The group called Pilgrims, by Pilgrim leader William Bradford, decided to go to Virginia. To do so, the Pilgrims had to make arrangements with one of the two companies that held charters to settle English lands. A charter was a document from the king giving a company the right to create a colony in North America. The London Virginia Company was in charge of all the land from what is now North Carolina north to the Hudson River. The Plymouth Virginia Company controlled all the land north of the Hudson.

The Pilgrims made an arrangement with the Plymouth Virginia Company. The company would supply money to finance the colony, and in exchange the Pilgrims would agree to give the company seven years of their labor.

The Plymouth Company investors did not feel there were enough Pilgrims to establish a successful colony so they recruited other people to join them. The Pilgrims had purchased their own small ship in Holland called the *Speedwell*. The company hired a larger ship called the *Mayflower*.

On August 4, 1620, the two ships set sail for North America and what was called New England. The plan was to sail to the mouth of the Hudson River and establish a colony. There were problems before the Pilgrims were out of sight of land. The *Speed-well* was leaking badly, and both ships turned back to Plymouth, England.

After another false start, it was decided to leave the *Speedwell* behind. As many Pilgrims as possible crammed into the *Mayflower* with the other colonists. Some people from the *Speedwell* were forced to stay in England. The *Mayflower* finally left England on September 6, 1620. There were 102 passengers on board. Thirty-five of the passengers had been part of the Leiden group. There were approximately 40 other Separatists from London who joined the Pilgrims. The other 25 or more passengers were not leaving England for religious reasons and were referred to as "Strangers" by the Pilgrims.

Despite their differences, the 102 colonists on the *Mayflower* would share the same fate and would all be referred to as Pilgrims by historians. It took more than two months to cross the Atlantic. During the trip, two people died. The first was one of the sailors. The other was William Butten, who had been the servant of one of the colonists. There was also one birth during the trip. Elizabeth Hopkins gave birth to a son. He was named Oceanus, in honor of

Mayflower

Little is known of the actual ship, the *Mayflower*, that brought the Pilgrims to Plymouth. However, extensive research has been done over the years to try to determine what the *Mayflower* looked like. It is known that the ship was a trading vessel that worked primarily in trading English goods for wine in Spain. It was not built for carrying passengers. The original records of the voyage give the tonnage of the ship and researchers determined the general dimensions of the *Mayflower* by comparing it to known ships of the same weight and time.

It is estimated that the *Mayflower* had an overall length of 90 feet with a keel of about 64 feet. It was about 26 feet wide. The hold of the ship would have been around 11 feet deep, and the space between decks where the 102 Pilgrims lived during the voyage was quite cramped.

In 1957, a group in England built a replica of the *Mayflower*. They then sailed it across the Atlantic, and it has been berthed in Plymouth, Massachusetts, ever since as a floating museum.

The Pilgrims sailed across the Atlantic Ocean on the *Mayflower* during a two-month journey. *(Library of Congress, Prints and Photographs Division [LC-D416-28072])*

his being born at sea. Despite their sailing during what is known now as hurricane season, the rest of the voyage was uneventful.

Land was first sighted on November 9, 1620. Two days later the *Mayflower* sailed into a small harbor. That harbor is now surrounded by Provincetown, Massachusetts, at the very tip of Cape Cod. The original destination of the *Mayflower* had been the Hudson River. However, because winter was fast approaching and the waters directly west and south of the Cape were very dangerous, it was decided to look for a spot nearby to spend the winter.

2

First Settlements in Massachusetts

PLYMOUTH COLONY

While the *Mayflower* remained anchored, the Pilgrim leaders decided that the group should agree to a set of rules. These rules became known as the Mayflower Compact, and all the men signed before they went ashore to explore. One group explored the area on foot, while another group assembled a small boat that had been stored in the *Mayflower*. The group on foot saw some Native Americans, but they were going away from the Pilgrims. It may be that the Native Americans were intentionally avoiding the Pilgrims because of the diseases that the European fishermen and explorers had already brought to New England.

The Pilgrims found a place where these Native Americans had stored corn and beans. The Pilgrims took the food and added it to their own supplies. When they returned to the *Mayflower*, the boat was ready and they began exploring what is now called Cape Cod Bay. The Pilgrims in the ship's boat crossed the bay and entered what would be called Plymouth Harbor. After spending two nights on an island, they landed at Plymouth Rock on December 11, 1620.

The area around the harbor had been cleared by the Pawtuxet band of the Wampanoag and had a number of open fields. The Pawtuxet had been wiped out by European diseases, and there was no one living in the immediate area. The Pilgrims decided that this was the best spot they had found. They returned to the *Mayflower* to

The Mayflower Compact

The Pilgrims' arrival at Cape Cod created a number of problems for the colonists. First, they were about to settle on land to which they had no claim. And second, they were outside the political jurisdiction of Virginia. While crossing the Atlantic, there had been problems between the Separatists (those seeking religious freedom) and the Strangers (colonists who had no religious reasons for going to the New World) on the *Mayflower*. According to an account written by one of the Pilgrim leaders, William Bradford, the Strangers were already making "mutinous speeches."

To prevent the situation from worsening, the Pilgrim leaders drew up a simple agreement by which Plymouth Colony would be governed. The document is known as the Mayflower Compact. It was signed by all the healthy men on November 21, 1620. This was after the *Mayflower* had landed on Cape Cod, but before the group had decided where to spend the winter.

The Mayflower Compact states that the colonists would "combine ourselves toge-

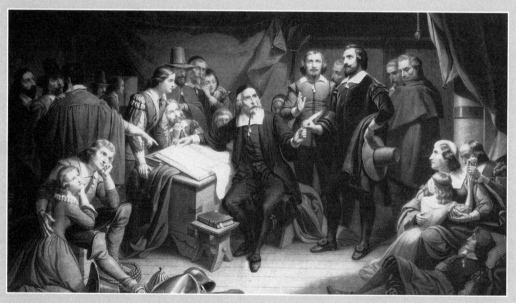

On November 21, 1620, all the healthy male Pilgrims signed the Mayflower Compact, a set of rules designed to help govern the new colony. *(Library of Congress, Prints and Photographs Division [LC-USZ61-206])*

ther into a civil body politick, for our better ordering and preservation." Out of necessity, the colonists began the first experiment in self-government by Europeans in North America. They agreed to allow the "civil body politick" to make laws. By signing the Mayflower Compact, they agreed to go along with the decisions of the majority. Because Plymouth Colony was so far from England and seemed so small and unimportant, it was left alone to experiment in democracy. So were other groups in other later colonies.

By the time England tried to assert more control, it was too late. Many of the colonists had already come to believe that they had the right to govern themselves.

◦‿‿◦

Mayflower Compact, 1620

Agreement Between the Settlers at New Plymouth: 1620

IN THE NAME OF GOD, AMEN. We, whose names are underwritten, the Loyal Subjects of our dread Sovereign Lord King James, by the Grace of God, of Great Britain, France, and Ireland, King, Defender of the Faith, &c. Having undertaken for the Glory of God, and Advancement of the Christian Faith, and the Honour of our King and Country, a Voyage to plant the first Colony in the northern Parts of Virginia; Do by these Presents, solemnly and mutually, in the Presence of God and one another, covenant and combine ourselves together into a civil Body Politick, for our better Ordering and Preservation, and Furtherance of the Ends aforesaid: And

by Virtue hereof do enact, constitute, and frame, such just and equal Laws, Ordinances, Acts, Constitutions, and Officers, from time to time, as shall be thought most meet and convenient for the general Good of the Colony; unto which we promise all due Submission and Obedience. IN WITNESS whereof we have hereunto subscribed our names at Cape-Cod the eleventh of November, in the Reign of our Sovereign Lord King James, of England, France, and Ireland, the eighteenth, and of Scotland the fifty-fourth, Anno Domini; 1620.

Mr. John Carver	Digery Priest
Mr. William Bradford	Thomas Williams
Mr Edward Winslow	Gilbert Winslow
Mr. William Brewster	Edmund Margesson
Isaac Allerton	Peter Brown
Myles Standish	Richard Britteridge
John Alden	George Soule
John Turner	Edward Tilly
Francis Eaton	John Tilly
James Chilton	Francis Cooke
John Craxton	Thomas Rogers
John Billington	Thomas Tinker
Joses Fletcher	John Ridgdale
John Goodman	Edward Fuller
Mr. Samuel Fuller	Richard Clark
Mr. Christopher Martin	Richard Gardiner
Mr. William Mullins	Mr. John Allerton
Mr. William White	Thomas English
Mr. Richard Warren	Edward Doten
John Howland	Edward Liest
Mr. Steven Hopkins	

tell the rest of the group. This was a moment of mixed feelings for William Bradford, one of the Pilgrim leaders. While he was off exploring, his wife had fallen overboard and drowned. Hers would be the first of many deaths that first winter. Before the group moved on to Plymouth, there were three more deaths and one birth. Peregrine White became the first British settler to be born in what would become Massachusetts.

As it was already the middle of December, there was little time to build proper shelters for the fast approaching winter. The Pilgrims built crude lean-tos and dug pits in the ground to live in. They also made a communal building with a thatched roof that soon filled up with sick people. Exposure to the cold New England winter and malnutrition weakened the Pilgrims. Soon most of them were sick and many died. On January 14, 1621, fire destroyed their communal building. The sick who had been inside were able to get out.

After exploring Cape Cod Bay in a small boat, the Pilgrims sailed the *Mayflower* across the bay and landed at Plymouth Rock on December 11, 1620. *(Library of Congress, Prints and Photographs Division [LC-USZ62-3461])*

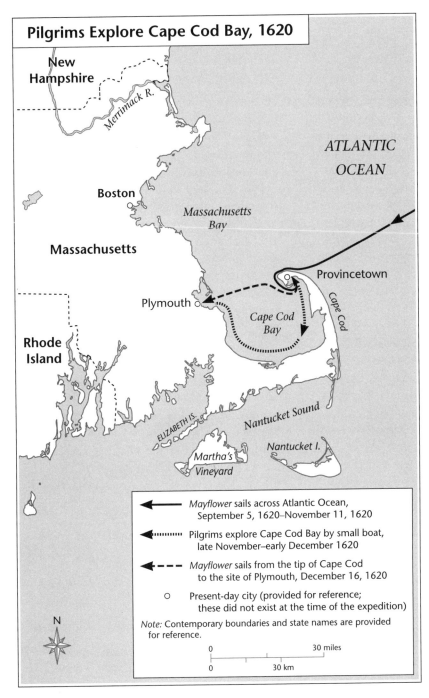

Pilgrims Explore Cape Cod Bay, 1620

New Hampshire

Merrimack R.

ATLANTIC OCEAN

Boston

Massachusetts Bay

Massachusetts

Provincetown

Plymouth

Cape Cod Bay

Cape Cod

Rhode Island

ELIZABETH IS.

Nantucket Sound

Martha's Vineyard

Nantucket I.

← *Mayflower* sails across Atlantic Ocean, September 5, 1620–November 11, 1620

◀········· Pilgrims explore Cape Cod Bay by small boat, late November–early December 1620

◀--- *Mayflower* sails from the tip of Cape Cod to the site of Plymouth, December 16, 1620

○ Present-day city (provided for reference; these did not exist at the time of the expedition)

Note: Contemporary boundaries and state names are provided for reference.

| 0 | | 30 miles |
| 0 | 30 km | |

N

After crossing the Atlantic Ocean on the *Mayflower,* the Pilgrims made landfall near the tip of Cape Cod. After exploring Cape Cod and Cape Cod Bay, they chose the site that became Plymouth, Massachusetts.

Squanto
(ca. 1580–1622)

In the early 1600s, before the Pilgrims landed in Plymouth, there were numerous voyages by different explorers along the North American coast. In 1614, John Smith sailed along the northeast coast. Historians believe that Squanto, or Tisquantum as he is sometimes called, of the Pawtuxet band of the Wampanoag in present-day Plymouth, was captured by Thomas Hunt. Hunt, an officer under Smith, ran Smith's fishing operation. Hunt decided to try to make a profit by capturing Native Americans. In 1615, Hunt tricked 20 or so Native Americans, including Squanto, into coming aboard his ship. Hunt then sailed off to the slave markets of Spain. Squanto was sold into slavery in Spain. He was later freed by an Englishman who took him to London, England, where he lived with an employee of the Newfoundland Company, Jim Slany.

Slany introduced Squanto to Sir Fernando Gorges, who was one of the main partners in the Plymouth Company. During his stay in London, Squanto learned to speak English. When Gorges planned a trip of exploration to North America, he hired Squanto to go along. Squanto was to be a guide and interpreter.

Gorges outfitted the expedition with Thomas Dermer as the captain. Dermer and Squanto sailed into the harbor where Squanto's village had been. They found that everyone there had died in 1617 of European-introduced disease. Squanto was the only member of the village still alive. Squanto stayed but ended up in a nearby Wampanoag village. Massasoit was the leader of this village. Massasoit and Squanto would play a major part in the survival of Plymouth Colony.

In the winter of 1621, a Native American, who had come down along the coast from Maine, walked into the Plymouth Colony. He is reported to have said in English, "Welcome, welcome Englishmen." His name was Samoset, and he had learned a little English from fishermen who had set up temporary camps along the Maine coast. Samoset told the Pilgrims of their nearby neighbors, the Wampanoag, and their great leader, Massasoit. The Pilgrims asked Samoset to make contact with Massasoit on their behalf.

At the worst time in the winter, there were only seven people healthy enough to gather firewood and feed the rest of the group. During that first winter, more than 40 Pilgrims died. Although the Pilgrims had seen Native Americans from a distance while exploring Cape Cod, they did not have any direct contact with them during their first winter in Plymouth.

Samoset left Plymouth and then returned on March 22 with Squanto, followed by Massasoit and numerous Wampanoag warriors. Squanto helped the Pilgrims negotiate a peace treaty with Massasoit and then stayed in Plymouth. Squanto was an enormous help to the Pilgrims. He taught them how to do many things. When the Pilgrims' attempts to plant English crops failed, Squanto helped them trade for Native American corn seed. He then showed them how to plant and fertilize it using fish. Squanto also helped the Pilgrims establish trade with Native Americans all around Massachusetts Bay.

Unfortunately, in November 1622, Squanto shared the fate of the rest of his village. He came down with a European disease and died. It is doubtful if the Pilgrims would have survived another winter without Squanto's help.

With Squanto as translator, Massasoit (shown here), grand sachem of all the Wampanoag bands, helped teach the Pilgrims how, where, and what to plant. *(Library of Congress, Prints and Photographs Division [LC-USZ62-120508])*

In February the Pilgrims found the nearby Wampanoag settlement but did not have any contact until later. On March 16, 1621, a member of the Abenaki tribe from what is now Maine, whose name was Samoset, entered the Pilgrim community. Samoset returned the next day with Squanto, a person who would become extremely important to the Pilgrims.

Squanto was the last living member of the Pawtuxet community that had lived at Plymouth. He had been captured by English explorers—from whom he had learned to speak English—and was away when the community had been wiped out by disease in 1617. Squanto would help the Pilgrims in many ways. First, he introduced them to Massasoit, the leader of the Wampanoag. Squanto served as the interpreter for the Pilgrims. Through Squanto, Massasoit gave the Pilgrims advice about how, where, and what to plant. Squanto arranged for the Pilgrims to trade for Native American seeds so they could plant fields of corn, beans, and squash.

Squanto also showed them the way Native Americans planted and tended their crops. Without the help of Squanto and Massasoit,

William Bradford
(1590–1657)

William Bradford was born in Austerfield in the Yorkshire section of England in 1590. His father died the year after his birth and his mother remarried. It was assumed that he would become a farmer like most of his relatives. He was also expected to study the Bible as part of his informal education. However, as William Bradford studied the Bible, he felt a sense of calling. Barely a teenager, he joined a group of Puritans who met in Scrooby at the home of William Brewster.

Many Puritans at the time were willing to remain in the Church of England while working to solve problems from within. For Brewster and his followers, that was not enough. They broke away from the church and were referred to as Separatists. Brewster was 24 years older than Bradford but considered him a brother in their religious group.

In 1609, William Bradford was put in jail for his religious beliefs. When he was released, he joined the rest of the group from Scrooby in leaving England for Leiden in the Netherlands. After 10 years there, William Bradford had become one of the leaders of the group. When some of the group decided to head off to North America and find a place where they could practice their religion the way they thought God wanted them to, Bradford was one of the leaders.

When the governor of Plymouth Colony, John Carver, died in the summer of 1621, William Bradford was elected governor. Bradford would remain as the governor of Plymouth Colony for the next 30 years. He was also a force throughout the New England colonies and was elected president of the New England Confederation twice when it was first established.

it is doubtful that the Pilgrims would have survived. The English crops of wheat and peas that they had brought and planted failed. Although there was abundant game, fish, and shellfish in the area, it would have been hard to survive a second winter without the Native American crops.

During the summer, John Carver, the governor of the colony, died while working in the fields. William Bradford was elected to succeed him and would remain governor of the colony for more than 30 years.

By fall 1621, the Pilgrims had built seven houses, a small fort, and a few other small buildings. Their storerooms were full of corn, beans, and squash. Governor Bradford felt the people of

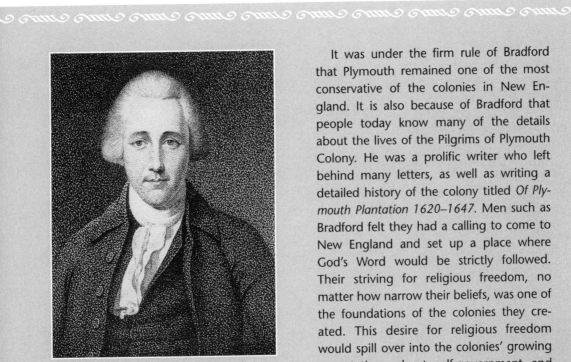

Elected in 1621, William Bradford governed Plymouth Colony for 30 years. *(Library of Congress, Prints and Photographs Division [LCUSZ61-625])*

It was under the firm rule of Bradford that Plymouth remained one of the most conservative of the colonies in New England. It is also because of Bradford that people today know many of the details about the lives of the Pilgrims of Plymouth Colony. He was a prolific writer who left behind many letters, as well as writing a detailed history of the colony titled *Of Plymouth Plantation 1620–1647*. Men such as Bradford felt they had a calling to come to New England and set up a place where God's Word would be strictly followed. Their striving for religious freedom, no matter how narrow their beliefs, was one of the foundations of the colonies they created. This desire for religious freedom would spill over into the colonies' growing expectations about self-government and personal freedom that would eventually lead to a war for independence from England.

Plymouth had much to be thankful for and called for a harvest feast to give thanks to God and to the help of their Native American neighbors. Many consider this to be the first Thanksgiving.

Although the Pilgrims seemed to be on good terms with Massasoit and the Wampanoag, they decided to fortify their village. Over the winter of 1621–22, they built a palisade (wooden wall made with pointed logs set upright) around the entire settlement.

In the years that followed, Plymouth Colony grew slowly. Children were born, and small numbers of new settlers came each year on supply ships from England. By 1626 there were just over 150 people living in Plymouth. The people of the colony soon developed a style of building that can still be seen in New England

In fall 1621, Governor Bradford called for a harvest feast to give thanks to God and to the colonists' Native American neighbors. Many of the Wampanoag were invited to the feast that has become known as the first Thanksgiving. *(Library of Congress, Prints and Photographs [LC-D416-90423])*

The First Thanksgiving

Harvest festivals have probably been a part of human tradition since the first people harvested a crop. They were common in Europe at the time the Pilgrims settled in Plymouth. These festivals celebrated the successful harvesting of the year's crops and were not held when crops were bad. The Pilgrims held a harvest festival in the fall of 1621 to celebrate the harvesting of their first crops at Plymouth Colony. The harvest would not have been possible without the help of Squanto, Massasoit, and the Pilgrims' Wampanoag neighbors. To acknowledge the importance of the help the colonists received from the Native Americans, Massasoit and many people from his village were invited to the festival.

Turkeys were quite plentiful around Plymouth at the time and were easily harvested by the colonists using their guns. There is no doubt that turkey was a major part of the menu at the first harvest festival in Plymouth. The Native Americans are said to have brought gifts of food, including venison, meat from deer, and other Native American staples.

The Pilgrims did not consider this harvest festival a religious day of thanksgiving. Those were days reserved for prayer that were called periodically. Thanksgiving days were often called after a group survived a disaster or in celebration of a victory. Two years after the first harvest festival, the Pilgrims declared a day of prayer and fasting because they were experiencing a severe drought. When it started to rain on that day, the community and church leaders changed it to a day of thanksgiving.

The first official American day of thanksgiving was called by the Continental Congress in 1777, when the American forces won the battle of Saratoga. The first national day of thanksgiving was declared by President George Washington in 1789, when the U.S. Constitution was ratified. In the early part of the 19th century, a number of states adopted a day in November for their thanksgiving holiday. Then, in the middle of the century, Sarah Josepha Hale, the editor of a magazine called *Godey's Lady's Book,* started a campaign to create a national day of thanksgiving as an annual event.

President Abraham Lincoln declared the next official Thanksgiving in 1863, during the Civil War, by making the last Thursday in November Thanksgiving Day. When the Civil War ended, Congress declared Thanksgiving a regular national holiday. As Thanksgiving became an established holiday, a number of traditions grew up around it. Many of them were related to the harvest festival that the Pilgrims had in 1621. Turkey and other traditional foods became common.

The idea of football games on Thanksgiving became popular in the first half of the 20th century. The custom of starting the Christmas shopping season on the day after Thanksgiving also grew in popularity. In 1939, President Franklin D.

(continues)

(continued)

Roosevelt moved Thanksgiving from the last Thursday in November to a week earlier. He did this at the suggestion of many large retailers who were hoping to extend the Christmas shopping season. Moving Thanksgiving created such an uproar that in 1941, the date of Thanksgiving was moved once again, to the fourth Thursday in November, where it remains today.

today. The next small group to set up a colony in what is now Massachusetts was the Dorchester Company. They set up a fishing outpost on Cape Ann, and the town of Salem was founded.

This original Cape Cod house was built in 1686 as a home for Jethro and Mary Coffin and is the oldest building on Nantucket Island in Massachusetts. *(Library of Congress, Prints & Photographs Division, HABS, [HABS, MASS, 10-NANT, 40-4])*

MASSACHUSETTS BAY COLONY

Many people in England who had been unhappy with the Church of England stayed members of the church and tried to change it from within. These people felt they were trying to purify the way the Church of England worshipped. These people were called Puritans. Many of them were members of Parliament. In 1625, James I, the king of England, died and was succeeded by Charles I. Charles I disbanded Parliament and began to persecute the Puritans.

For one group of Puritans, the example set by the Separatists in Plymouth seemed to be the best solution to their problems in England. This new group was led by John Winthrop and was much better organized and financed than the Plymouth Colony. Winthrop had been a successful lawyer and owned a family estate known as Groton Manor. Winthrop was concerned by the situation in England. Not only was Charles I opposed to the Puritans, the economic situation at the time was making it hard for landowners to prosper.

Winthrop used his own wealth and connections to become a partner in the Massachusetts Bay Company. The purpose of the company was to create a Puritan colony in and around Massachusetts Bay. Winthrop believed it would be better for himself and his family if they joined the new colony and created a place where they could practice their Puritan religion without interference from the king. By the time they set sail for Massachusetts in 1630, they had already scouted out the lands they were going to settle and had more than 1,000 people with them.

Just because they were better organized than the first settlers at Plymouth did not mean the new Massachusetts Bay Colony would not face problems and hardships. When Winthrop and the colonists arrived at Cape Ann in the summer of 1630, they

King of Scotland from infancy, King James I inherited the English throne when Elizabeth I died in 1603, and he ruled England and Ireland until his death in 1625. *(Library of Congress, Prints and Photographs Division [LC-USZ26-105812])*

found that the members of the Dorchester Company had taken the best open land sites for themselves. It would be many years before the colonists could effectively create new farmland from the surrounding forest. Their first home sites were often along the rivers and bays of the area where natural open land already existed.

The members of the Massachusetts Bay Colony soon spread out from Cape Ann to lands along the Charles and the Mystic Rivers in what are today the cities of Charlestown, Boston, Cambridge, and Watertown. It was difficult for Winthrop to keep track of all his colonists with them spread out over what was then a roadless wilderness.

Even though Massachusetts Bay Colony was much better organized and supplied, the first winter was still extremely hard

Puritans and Their Beliefs

The people who came from England to Plymouth and Massachusetts Bay Colonies were considered part of the Puritan movement. However, defining exactly what that was has always been a challenge for historians. On the surface, it looks like a difference of opinion between the Church of England and some of its parishioners who disagreed with the way the church practiced religion. In part, this is true. When Henry VIII split the Church of England from the Catholic Church, it retained many Catholic traditions.

As time went on, many people in England wanted the church to conform more to the Protestant doctrines that had developed as a result of the Reformation. The Reformation had been an action by a number of people who were dissatisfied with the Catholic Church and in protest set up their own churches. This is where the term Protestant comes from. As Protestant thought expanded, many within the Church of England felt that there was a need for serious reform. These people wanted a stricter interpretation of the Bible and all remaining vestiges of Catholicism removed. In their minds, the Church of England needed to be purified. It was from this idea that the term Puritan evolved.

The Puritans saw the church as divided into two parts. One part consisted of attending church and trying to live a life that would earn them salvation. They considered this the visible church. The other part consisted of those "saintly" members of the church who had earned salvation and a place in heaven in the next life. This was thought of as the invisible church.

for people. In Plymouth, almost half the people had died the first winter. In the Massachusetts Bay Colony, around 20 percent, or about 200 people, died of disease and malnutrition. The colonists had shipped enough food to get them through the first winter, but much of it had spoiled while crossing the Atlantic. When the first supply ships arrived the following spring, a number of colonists decided to return to England.

Despite the difficulty of the first winter and the departure of almost 200 more settlers, Massachusetts Bay Colony continued to grow and become prosperous. The colony had to figure out what they had to trade and who they could trade with. The most readily available resource was wood. The vast forests of New England came right to the edge of the ocean in most places. There was an

The idea of being a part of the invisible church is what set the Puritans apart from the rest of the society. For them it was not enough just to go to church on Sunday. They felt that people needed to live a life of piety and moral correctness every day. Some groups of Puritans, such as the Pilgrims who settled Plymouth Colony, withdrew from the Church of England and set up their own religious groups. These Separatists were persecuted by English authorities. Other Puritans, such as John Winthrop, remained within the church until Charles I came to the throne.

In New England, the Puritans used their beliefs not only to set up churches the way they wanted them but also as the ruling principles of the colonies. In the early years of the Plymouth and Massachusetts Bay colonies, what existed was a theocracy, where the church and the state were one. One had to prove oneself a true member of the "invisible church" to vote and be considered a member of the community. The Puritan ideals of the colonies' founders made for a very strict society that punished people for infractions against the religious doctrines as well as crimes against the society as a whole.

It was this intolerance that brought about the exile of people such as Roger Williams and Anne Hutchinson. It also resulted in the liberal use of the stocks (wooden restraints that people were put into for punishment) and eventually led to the witch hunts in Salem and throughout Massachusetts. Many aspects of Puritan thought have lingered into modern times. Until recently, many states had laws against doing business or selling alcohol on Sundays. There are many other restrictions on behavior that often seem out of place in our more tolerant times.

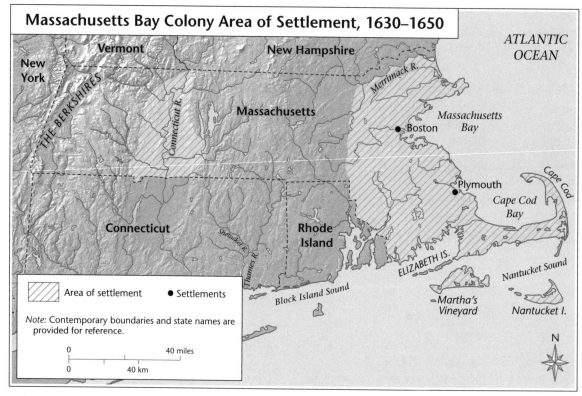

Massachusetts Bay Colony Area of Settlement, 1630–1650

ATLANTIC OCEAN

Vermont

New Hampshire

New York

THE BERKSHIRES

Connecticut R.

Merrimack R.

Massachusetts

Massachusetts Bay

Boston

Plymouth

Cape Cod

Cape Cod Bay

Connecticut

Shetucket R.

Thames R.

Rhode Island

ELIZABETH IS.

Nantucket Sound

Block Island Sound

Martha's Vineyard

Nantucket I.

Area of settlement ● Settlements

Note: Contemporary boundaries and state names are provided for reference.

0   40 miles
0   40 km

N

Early settlement in Massachusetts took place within 30 miles of the coast and in the Connecticut River Valley.

abundance of fish in the waters around the colony. The colony was also soon producing more cattle and other farm products than it could consume.

England really did not need these products. The English produced their own food and could trade for fish and lumber with the Baltic countries, which were much closer. The colonists put some of the lumber to good use by building their own ships, and then they began trading with the islands of the Caribbean. The islands had been settled by people from many of the countries of Europe, and most were involved in producing single crops such as sugar on large plantations worked by slaves. In a very short period of time, Massachusetts Bay Colony became the primary trading partner of many of the sugar plantations in the islands. As trade grew, so did the port towns of the colony. Boston has one of the best natural harbors in the world, and it quickly became the most important trading center. It also became the capital of the colony and remains the state capital today. This trading relationship gave the colony economic independence from England.

In addition to their economic independence, the leaders of the colony also believed they had religious independence and a certain amount of political freedom. Although the leaders of the colony were pleased with the progress, the king was concerned. Not only had the colony left the Church of England, the king was not collecting any revenue on their trade and prosperity.

To remedy this situation, in 1634, Charles I wanted to revoke the colony's charter. John Winthrop refused to return the charter. Instead, he ordered out the militia and fortified Boston Harbor as much as possible. Winthrop and the other Puritan leaders recognized that England legally owned the land their colony had settled. However, they had come to New England to worship and live as

Anne Dudley Bradstreet
(1612–1672)

Anne Dudley Bradstreet came to America with her husband, Simon Bradstreet, on the same ship from England as had John Winthrop and her father, Thomas Dudley. Her father, and later her husband, served as governor of the colony. Bradstreet had been educated at home in England, and she became America's first published poet. Her brother-in-law, Reverend John Woodbridge, returned to England in 1647 and carried with him copies of some of Bradstreet's poems. He had them published anonymously in London in 1650.

The collection of poems was entitled *The Tenth Muse, Lately Sprung Up in America,* and it was well received in both England and in America. The poems are not only noteworthy for being the first by someone living in America but also for the glimpse into the early years of life in Massachusetts as a Puritan. Many of her poems deal with the struggles of life. In later poems, she wrote about the anxiety of birthing her eight children, the deaths of her grandchildren, and the 1666 fire that destroyed her house and beloved library. There are also a number of long poems that deal with the religious side of her life as a Puritan. In 1666, Bradstreet revised her poems, and a second edition was published in Boston by her family after her death in 1672.

Cod

By the time the Pilgrims established their colony at Plymouth, Europeans had been coming to New England for many years. Some came to explore the region and map out the coastlines of the territories claimed by a variety of European governments. Others came to fish, and the fish they were most interested in was cod.

The Atlantic cod were extremely abundant in the waters off the northeast coast of North America. Cod were easily caught in the relatively shallow water of the Grand Banks of Newfoundland and Labrador and Georges Bank off the coast of Massachusetts. Basque fishermen, from what is now the Basque region of Spain, had perfected the technique of drying cod using salt, which made it possible for the fish to be transported great distances to be sold. Along with the Basque came fishermen from England, France, and Portugal.

The fishermen would set up temporary camps along the coast, where they would dry the cod they caught. Once they had a boatload, they would sail back to Europe and sell their dried cod. The colonists in Massachusetts saw the possibilities of creating their own fishing trade. A salt works that extracted salt from ocean water was one of the early businesses set up in Boston Harbor. One of John Winthrop's sons started the salt works, so the colonists would not have to buy salt in the Caribbean. Cod became the cornerstone of the trade with sugar plantations of the Caribbean. The plantations were farmed using slave labor, and dried cod was a relatively cheap food for the plantation owners to feed the slaves.

The colonists traded the cod, along with forest products and excess produce from their farms, for molasses and sugar. At first they traded the molasses and sugar in Europe for manufactured goods they could not make themselves. Later the merchants of New England learned they could make a greater profit by turning much of the sugar products from the Caribbean into rum. This allowed certain descendants of the Puritans and Pilgrims to become very wealthy.

they chose and were not going to give in to the king without a fight. The king backed down, and Massachusetts Bay Colony continued to go forward.

The leaders of the colony knew that for the colony to continue to grow, people would need to be educated. In 1635, the first public school in North America was opened. The Boston Latin School was supported by the people of Boston and continues today as one of the top public high schools in the country. The following year,

1636, the colony set up a college to train ministers for their churches in the community that would be called Cambridge. One of the colonists, John Harvard, donated his personal library of 300 books and a considerable fortune to the college. This was America's first college and soon became known as Harvard College, after its benefactor.

During the early years of the colony, many good things were happening, but there were also problems. The largest problem the

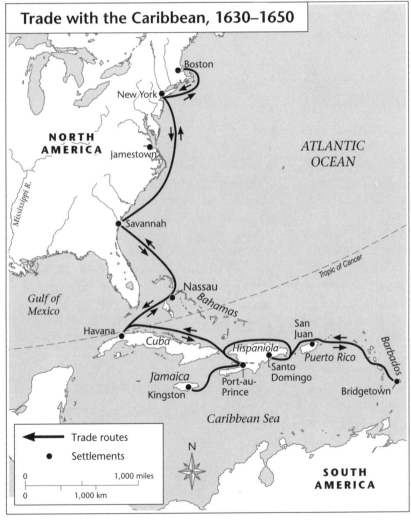

Trade with the Caribbean, 1630–1650

Merchants from Boston were soon trading by ship with the English colonies in North America and with many of the sugar plantations in the Caribbean.

colony faced was that many of the people who were settling there were not Puritans. The rules of the colony allowed only "freemen" to vote. Freemen had to be members of a Puritan church, and it was difficult to become a member. Also, the freemen felt that the leaders of the colony were not giving them all the rights they were entitled to by the colony's charter. To solve these problems, John Winthrop, as governor, did two things. First, he made sure that the freemen received all the rights that the charter had granted them. Then voting rights were given to all male property owners in the colony.

Even though the Puritans came to Massachusetts, in part, to worship as they pleased, they were not tolerant of people who did

Harvard

The Puritans who settled Massachusetts Bay Colony included many people who had been well educated in England. Many of the leaders and clergy in the group had attended colleges such as Oxford and Cambridge in England. So it is not surprising that just six years after they arrived, they wanted to create a college that the young men of the colony could attend.

In 1636, the Great and General Court of the Massachusetts Bay Colony voted to establish a college. It was decided to locate the college across the Charles River from Boston, in a community that was called Newtowne. It was not long before the community felt that the home of North America's first college should have a loftier sounding name. Newtowne was changed to Cambridge, after the town in England where Cambridge University is located.

The college appears to have been nameless until 1638. At that time, John Harvard, who was a young minister in Charlestown, died and left his library and half his estate to the college. To memorialize his gift, the school took his name and was called Harvard College until 1780, when it became Harvard University. The original goal of the college was to provide well-educated ministers, who would continue to guide the colony as its Puritan founders had planned. Most of the prominent men of colonial Massachusetts attended Harvard. Many did become ministers, while others became lawyers, merchants, and politicians.

In 1653, John Sassamon, a Native American, studied at Harvard. He was killed while trying to help the colonists during King Philip's War. It would not be until 1879 that women were allowed to study at Harvard as members of the separate Radcliffe College.

not follow the rules or who disagreed with them. Stocks were set up in the center of every community in the colony. A stock was a device used to hold a person immobile while the passing community members would humiliate them by yelling, spitting, and sometimes throwing things at the person placed in the stocks. Some stocks held the person by his or her head and arms or by the arms and legs. Some stocks even had a place for the head, arms, and legs. The first person to be put in the stocks in Boston was the carpenter who built them. His crime had been overcharging the town leaders.

Dissenters were another problem the colony faced. These were people who disagreed with the religious and political practices of

This reproduction of an engraving by Paul Revere shows Harvard University, America's first college.
(Library of Congress, Prints and Photographs Division [LC-USZ62-96223])

Stocks were used in the colonies as a form of punishment. These stocks are a reconstruction at Colonial Williamsburg in Virginia. *(Library of Congress, Prints and Photographs Division [LC-USZ62-97883])*

the Puritans. Roger Williams was one of the most vocal. He disagreed with the fact that the colony's government and church leadership were one and the same. He felt that people should not be told how to worship. He also disagreed with the way the colonists dealt with the Native Americans. Many people just took land without worrying about any Native American claims. Williams felt that the colonists should pay the Native Americans for their land.

Anne Marbury Hutchinson
(1591–1643)

Anne Marbury Hutchinson was the daughter of an English minister who had shared his radical beliefs with his daughter. After Hutchinson married, she and her family attended the church of John Cotton in England. When Cotton left and went to Massachusetts to join the Puritans, Anne Hutchinson and her family followed in 1634.

A common practice at the time was for groups of women to meet during the week to read scripture and discuss the sermon that they had heard on the previous Sunday. Shortly after her arrival in Boston, Hutchinson was regularly hosting such a group. This would not have been a problem except that Hutchinson began sharing some of her radical thoughts with the group. She was also attracting more and more people, including Governor Henry Vane. Hutchinson, probably in part because of the teachings of her father, had a number of religious ideas that were in conflict with Puritan teachings.

Foremost among them was the idea that only faith was needed to achieve salvation. This theory was called a "covenant of faith." The Puritans believed in a "covenant of work" where the way someone behaved was the path to salvation. As the group at Hutchinson's grew, so did the concern of John Winthrop and other Puritan leaders. Hutchinson allowed her brother-in-law, John Wheelwright, to preach his equally radical ideas, after he had been denied the ministry of a church. This contributed to the fear the establishment had of her. A group of church leaders, referred to as a synod, condemned her ideas in 1637.

Then, in civil court, Governor Winthrop pressed the case against Hutchinson, and it was brought to trial. During her trial, Winthrop served as both judge and prosecutor. Hutchinson adroitly avoided being trapped into a confession of wrongdoing while Winthrop cross-examined her for hours. Finally, she made a statement that the court could use against her. Hutchinson claimed that her testimony was a direct revelation from God. In the eyes of the Puritans, this was heresy. Hutchinson was convicted and banished by the court and excommunicated by the synod. Wheelwright had been banished earlier. He went north and founded the town of Exeter, New Hampshire. Hutchinson and her family went south to Rhode Island, where they joined Roger Williams's colony.

When it seemed that the Puritans of Boston were starting to have an influence in Rhode Island, the Hutchinsons moved again. This time, they settled in the Dutch colony of New Amsterdam in the town of Pelham Bay on Long Island. In 1643, Anne Hutchinson and five of her children were killed by Native Americans.

Williams was arrested and was going to be sent back to England. John Winthrop intervened on his behalf, and instead Williams left the colony and moved to what would become Rhode Island. Anne Hutchinson was another dissenter who challenged the authority of the Puritan churches. She too was banished and joined Williams's new colony in Rhode Island.

In the first 10 years of the colony, more than 20,000 people came from England. The majority of these people were not Puritans. They were people who were leaving England to escape the economic and political problems that England faced at the time. The rapid growth of Massachusetts made conflict with Native Americans unavoidable.

Colonists and Native Americans

THE PEQUOT WAR

The cooperation between Native Americans and colonists that had saved the Plymouth Colony did not last. Problems between the two groups quickly became serious. As more and more people arrived in Massachusetts, they were encouraged to spread out up and down the coast. There were soon settlements north into what is now Maine and south into what would become Connecticut. In Connecticut, the settlers quickly spread out up the Connecticut River into territory that belonged to the Pequot tribe. Saybrook was established at the mouth of the river with a substantial fort. The communities of Wethersfield, Hartford, and Windsor, in what would become Connecticut and Springfield in Massachusetts, were all settled along the river before the first major conflict with the Native Americans.

Both the leaders in Boston and those in the small Connecticut colony saw the advantage in taking over the fertile lands of the Connecticut River Valley. They knew they would have to deal with the Pequot to do it. At first, they used the Pequot as trading partners. The colonists exchanged cloth and metal objects for furs. However, the Pequot had fought with many of their Native American neighbors before and after the coming of the English. They were not going to let more of their land be taken without a fight. As more and more settlers moved into Pequot territory it was inevitable that there would be conflict.

The first strike in what would become known as the Pequot War is not clearly recorded. The leaders of the Massachusetts Colony considered the death of Captain John Stone in 1634, a trader of uncertain reputation, as the first strike in the war. Stone was killed by the Western Niantic, who were allies of the Pequot. The leaders of the colony used the death of Stone as the reason to force the Pequot to sign a treaty with the colony that was unfavorable to them. Two years later, when another trader, John Oldham, was killed by Native Americans on or near Block Island off the coast of what became Rhode Island, Massachusetts sent an expedition of 90 men led by John Endecott to get revenge.

It is not known if the Narragansett living on Block Island had anything to do with Oldham's death. Pequot were believed to have hijacked the boat. This did not matter to Endecott's force. They burned a number of Narragansett villages on Block Island and then crossed over to Connecticut to search out any Pequot who had been involved. The colonists at Saybrook were very upset that the force from Massachusetts had been sent to deal with the Pequot. They feared that if the Pequot were attacked by Endecott and his men, they would suffer the reprisals.

Endecott did not listen to the people of Saybrook and attacked several Pequot villages. They burned the villages and killed one Native American. Sassacus, the Pequot leader, did as the people of Saybrook feared and sought revenge. In the winter of 1636–37, Sassacus and the Pequot attacked the fort at Saybrook and a number of smaller settlements. In spring 1637, the Pequot attacked Wethersfield and killed nine colonists.

The costs to the Pequot for these attacks were devastating. A large colonial army was gathered under the command of Captains John Underhill and John Mason. In addition to a large force of colonists, many Native Americans joined in. The colonists used the traditional rivalries among the Native American groups to recruit allies. Mohegan, Narragansett, and Niantic warriors fought alongside the colonists. On May 26, 1637, the combined forces attacked Sassacus's village at what is today Mystic, Connecticut. At first, the Pequot were able to repel their attackers from behind their palisades. However, the colonists and their allies set the village on fire. The Pequot who

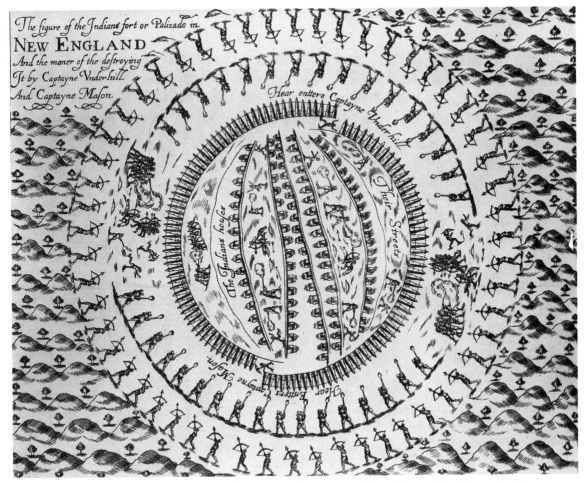

First published in a 1638 book, this illustration depicts the Pequot village that a colonial army led by Captains John Underhill and John Mason attacked in 1637. *(Library of Congress, Prints and Photographs Division [LC-USZ62-32055])*

tried to escape were killed; those who stayed behind died in the flames. Somewhere between 500 and 1,000 Pequot, mostly women, children, and old men, died during the battle.

Sassacus and many of his warriors had fled. They were found in July in a swamp west of New Haven and were attacked again. This time when Sassacus escaped he fled to the territory of the Mohawk. The Mohawk did not want to appear to be on Sassacus's side. They beheaded him and let the colonists know they would no longer have to fear the Pequot leader.

Atrocities against Native Americans

From the earliest explorers who kidnapped Native Americans through the Seven Years' War, which ended in 1763, the people of Massachusetts and the other colonies treated the people they found already living there terribly. The early explorers often kidnapped Native Americans to bring back to England as novelties and curiosities to be displayed and/or sold into slavery. Squanto's story is just one example of this. Fortunately for Squanto, he made it back to his home—most did not.

The fate of Squanto's village in what would become Plymouth is another example of the pain and suffering Europeans caused Native Americans. The people of Squanto's village were wiped out by European diseases while he was away. In this case, it was inadvertent. In other cases, Native Americans were intentionally given blankets and clothing that had been used by sick and/or dying colonists in hopes of infecting them with diseases that were often fatal.

The Puritans felt that it was their destiny from God to create a Puritan paradise in Massachusetts. Since the Native Americans had their own religious beliefs that were very different from the Puritans', they were considered heathens and savages. The Puritans and most other colonists believed that they had a right to take the Native American lands in any way necessary. People of European descent who felt that Native Americans should be treated justly, such as Roger Williams, were cast out of the Puritan communities. In battles between the colonists and Native Americans, the colonists often slaughtered women and children when they captured a village. When they did not murder their captives, the colonists would often sell the Native Americans as slaves to the plantation owners in the Caribbean.

The attitudes of the Puritans set the stage for the annihilation of Native Americans throughout the 17th, 18th, and 19th centuries. Even today, more than 100 years after the last armed conflict, Native Americans often do not have the same opportunities as white Americans. The vast majority of Native Americans live on isolated reservations where the schools, housing, and other services are substandard. Despite the many accomplishments of the Puritans and others in the English colonies, the treatment of Native Americans was deplorable.

The Pequot who survived were rounded up and became slaves. The colonists gave some of the Pequot to their Native American allies as payment for their help. Other Pequot were sold in the slave markets of the Caribbean. A few Pequot avoided capture and escaped. These Pequot joined the tribes that were willing to take them in. The colonists had effectively wiped out the Pequot and stopped the use of Pequot tribal and place-names. Almost 20 years later, in 1655, the colonists freed the remaining Pequot slaves in New England and allowed them to return to the site of their village on the Mystic River.

The way the colonists dealt with the Pequot was very upsetting to many of the other Native Americans in New England. Many Pequot had been slaughtered by the colonists even as they were trying to surrender. After the Pequot War, the Native Americans of New England were wary of the colonists who kept arriving in larger and larger numbers each year.

THE NEW ENGLAND CONFEDERATION

By 1643 there were a number of English colonies in New England, each with its own government. Massachusetts was the largest, but Plymouth was still a separate colony. Connecticut and Rhode Island had been established along with a colony at New Haven that would later become part of Connecticut. All these colonies shared concerns about conflicts with their Native American neighbors.

The colonies needed more and more land to support their fast growing populations. Sometimes, treaties were made where Native Americans were paid for the loss of their land. However, much of the time colonists would just take any land they wanted. Realizing that additional conflicts were likely, the leaders of the New England colonies decided to form an alliance for their protection.

The colonies agreed to help defend each other and formed the New England Confederation. Although the confederation lasted for more than 40 years, there was often rivalry among the colonies. The leaders of Massachusetts thought they should have more of a say because their colony was by far the largest. The others thought each colony should be represented equally. This is an argument that would continue in one way or another until the U. S. Constitution was adopted.

The New England Confederation clearly recognized the independence of all its members in the running of their colonies. What they agreed to do was help each other in military matters. In 1675 the New England Confederation was put to its most serious test.

KING PHILIP'S WAR

By 1670 there were more than 50,000 non-Indian people in New England, where 50 years earlier there had been none. Their settlements stretched out along the coast from what is now Maine to the border between Connecticut and New York. In Connecticut, colonists had moved up the Connecticut River valley into western Massachusetts. This rapid population growth created a great deal of tension in New England.

Primary among these tensions was the need for land. The Native Americans who inhabited the land before the English came

Metacom, or King Philip, became chief of the Wampanoag in 1662. *(Library of Congress, Prints and Photographs Division [LC-USZ62-96234])*

obviously had first claim to it. However, England claimed the whole area as part of its empire. This was also complicated by border disputes between the four colonies of Massachusetts, Plymouth, Rhode Island, and Connecticut. Along the frontiers of the colonies, settlers often just took what they wanted and defended it as best they could.

In addition to the colonists' greed for more and more of the lands claimed by the various tribes in New England, there was an underlying racial intolerance on the part of the English colonists. Even Native Americans who had been converted to Christianity, called "Praying Indians" at the time, and who fought alongside the colonists were treated as inferior citizens.

King Philip's War was the unavoidable outcome of this conflict between cultures and races. Metacom, also called Metacomet, or King Philip as the English called him, was the leader of the Wampanoag. He was the second son of Massasoit, the Wampanoag leader who had befriended and helped the Pilgrims at Plymouth. His story and the account of the rebellion he led against the colonists of New England shows the roots of the mistreatment of Native Americans that continues to this day.

Unlike Massasoit, his sons saw the colonists as a threat on many levels. The settlers continued to take Wampanoag land and fought among themselves over who had the right to control the sale of Native American lands. After Massasoit died, his eldest son, Wamsutta, became the leader, or sachem, of the Wampanoag. As the leader of the tribe, he negotiated land sales to Rhode Island. Under the leadership of Roger Williams, Rhode Island probably had the best relationship with its Native American neighbors of all the colonies.

The leaders of Plymouth Colony did not want to see Rhode Island gain any more land, especially where it encroached on lands that they claimed. Plymouth sent out a small force of men, led by Major Josiah Wilson, to get Wamsutta and bring him to Plymouth, where they planned to convince him that he had to sell land only to them. During his captivity in Plymouth, Wamsutta became sick, and he died on his way home.

On the death of Wamsutta, Metacom became the leader of the Wampanoag. He was angered over the death of his brother, believing that Wamsutta had been poisoned by his captors. Metacom entered into a plot to drive the colonists back into the sea from which they came. He sent representatives to tribes throughout the area hoping to build a coalition of Native Americans. In January 1675, the rumors of a Native American uprising became believable for the colonists when a Praying Indian named John Sassamon reported to the governor of Plymouth Colony, Josiah Winslow, that Metacom was preparing for war.

After reporting to Governor Winslow, John Sassamon was murdered. Metacom denied having any part in the murder. However, three Native Americans were captured, charged with the crime, and executed. Throughout the remainder of winter 1675, Wampanoag, Pocumtuc, and Nipmuc warriors attacked small settlements throughout the colonies. The outlying settlements, especially those in western Massachusetts in the Connecticut River Valley, felt the brunt of the early stages of the war.

In the meantime, the colonies had forced the Narragansett to sign a treaty in which they agreed to turn over all Wampanoag who might seek refuge with the Narragansett. In December 1675, Governor Winslow led a large force into Narragansett territory to make sure they were not harboring any Wampanoag. Without further

This scene shows the colonists of Hadley, Massachusetts, rallying to fight the nearby Algonquian nations. This skirmish was one of many fought during King Philip's War. *(Library of Congress, Prints and Photographs Division [LC-USZ62-75122])*

negotiation or proof that the Narragansett had violated the treaty, Winslow's forces began burning Narragansett villages. On December 19, 1675, Winslow reached the Narragansett's main village, which sat on high ground in the middle of the Great Swamp, which is near the current town of West Kingston, Rhode Island.

Normally, this village was a well-defended spot with water all around it. However, the winter of 1675–76 had already been a cold one, and the colonists' forces were able to reach the village over the frozen swamp. It has been estimated that 300 Narragansett warriors and an equal number of women and children were killed on that day. There was no evidence then or now that the Narragansett were ever allied with Metacom. The guerrilla warfare of the Native Americans was met with large forces of colonists and their Praying Indian allies, killing any Native Americans they could find.

It soon became obvious that King Philip's War was going to be the end of any hopes of Native Americans' hanging on to any

Originally published in *Harper's Magazine* in 1857 and quite partial to the colonists involved in the incident, this engraving illustrates the colonists' taking of a Narragansett village in the Great Swamp of Rhode Island in December 1675. *(Library of Congress, Prints and Photographs Division [LC-USZ62-97115])*

Sudbury, Massachusetts, was just one of the many settlements involved in King Philip's War. This engraving, again partial to the colonists, appeared in *Harper's Magazine* in June 1857. *(Library of Congress, Prints and Photographs Division [LC-USZ62-77028])*

power in New England. Metacom was betrayed, and the colonists with their Native American allies trapped him in a swamp near New Hope, Rhode Island. When Metacom's body was finally found among the fallen, the colonial commander, Captain Church, ordered that Metacom be decapitated and the remainder of his body cut in quarters. The head was returned to Plymouth, where it was put on public display.

In the end, more than 5,000 Native Americans and more than 2,500 colonists died during King Philip's War. Many captured Native Americans were transported to the Caribbean and sold as slaves. It has been estimated that these numbers represented 40 percent of the Native Americans and 5 percent of the whites in New England at the time. If that is the case, then, in terms of percentage, King Philip's War was the bloodiest ever fought by North Americans. From that point forward, the relations between colonists—and later the United States—and Native Americans was one of sending in the military first and then making peace with the survivors if there were any. However, ending any possible threat to the colonies from Native Americans was not the end of the problems the colonies faced.

4

Revolution, Reform, and Restoration in England

The rule of King Charles I was a time of many problems in England. In 1629, Charles dissolved the English Parliament when it refused to give him the resources that he needed to fight a war with Scotland. There were many Puritans in Parliament, including John Winthrop. The Puritans also objected to Charles's plan to return the Church of England as the only English Church. Many refer to this time as the Great Migration, when thousands of Puritan and non-Puritan English people fled the chaos in England for the American colonies.

Charles I recalled Parliament in 1640, only to dismiss it after just three weeks. Later that year, Charles I recalled Parliament again. This Parliament would stay in session for the next 13 years, during one of the darkest times in modern English history. The Puritans in Parliament and throughout the country rose up against Charles I, and a civil war began in 1642.

The Puritans in the English Civil War were called Roundheads because they wore their hair in a close-cropped fashion that was in keeping with the simple dress that the Puritans adopted. The king's followers wore their hair long and were referred to as Cavaliers, a term that had been used in the past to describe mounted knights.

Oliver Cromwell rose to the top of the Puritan army and proved to be a very capable military leader. His New Model Army won a number of victories and eventually defeated the forces of the king. Charles I was tried and executed for treason on January 30, 1649. After defeating the Catholic and royalist forces in Ireland and Scotland, Oliver Cromwell became the Lord Protector of England. During the English Civil War, the colonies had been left to themselves and had developed ways of governing themselves. In Massachusetts, the town meeting became the prominent form of government. The voting members of the community would gather and make decisions for the town. This is a practice that still exists in many small New England towns.

After the victory of the Puritans in England, there was a period of reverse migration, when large numbers of people went back to England to be a part of the Puritan country that was being created. Many leaders in New England were concerned that England would become the place of Puritan power, and it would affect the way they lived and worshipped.

Shown in a reproduction of a painting by Robert Walker, Oliver Cromwell was a Puritan and military leader who eventually became Lord Protector of England. *(Library of Congress, Prints and Photographs Division [LC-USZ62-95711])*

In England, Cromwell and his advisers saw that trade with the colonies in North America had suffered. Due to the turmoil of the English Civil War and the disruption in trade it had caused, many traders in North America and especially those in Massachusetts had begun trading with the French and the Dutch in the Caribbean and Europe. To bring trade with the colonies back under control of England, Parliament passed the first Navigation Act in 1651. The part of this law that most affected the merchants of Massachusetts stated that colonies could only trade with England.

Many believe that the Navigation Act of 1651, as well as the additions to it over the next 40 years, had two consequences. First, some merchants continued to trade as they had, in defiance of the

English laws. Other merchants obeyed the law but felt it was unfair. Although the importance of the Navigation Acts in eventually bringing about the American Revolution is probably minimal, they did contribute to a sense of defiance toward England.

Although Cromwell's victories were in part a victory for the rising middle classes in England, the country was not really ready for the strict ideals of the Puritans. When Cromwell died in 1658, his son took over as Lord Protector. He lasted only nine months in the job before he resigned, and a battle began to restore Charles II, Charles I's son, to the throne.

Town meetings have played an important role in New England government since the gatherings' colonial roots. At this early 20th-century town meeting in Pelham, Massachusetts, citizens prepare to vote on how to spend tax money. *(Library of Congress, Prints and Photographs Division [LC-USZ62-84294])*

Excerpt from the Navigation Act of 1651

For the increase of the shipping and the encouragement of the navigation of this nation, which under the good providence and protection of God is so great a means of the welfare and safety of this Commonwealth: be it enacted by this present Parliament, and the authority thereof, that from and after the first day of December, one thousand six hundred fifty and one, and from thence forwards, no goods or commodities whatsoever of the growth, production or manufacture of Asia, Africa or America, or of any part thereof; or of any islands belonging to them, or which are described or laid down in the usual maps or cards of those places, as well of the English plantations as others, shall be imported or brought into this Commonwealth of England, or into Ireland, or any other lands, islands, plantations, or territories to this Commonwealth belonging, or in their possession, in any other ship or ships, vessel or vessels whatsoever, but only in such as do truly and without fraud belong only to the people of this Commonwealth, or the plantations thereof, as the proprietors or right owners thereof; and whereof the master and mariners are also for the most part of them of the people of this Commonwealth, under the penalty of the forfeiture and loss of all the goods that shall be imported contrary to this act; as also of the ship (with all her tackle, guns and apparel) in which the said goods or commodities shall be so brought in and imported; the one moiety to the use of the Commonwealth, and the other moiety to the use and behoof of any person or persons who shall seize the goods or commodities, and shall prosecute the same in any court of record within this Commonwealth.

After a number of battles, Charles II's forces prevailed and the monarchy was restored. Charles II would rule as king of England, Scotland, and Ireland for the next 25 years. At the restoration of the monarchy, many Puritans fled to the colonies. This was a period of relative stability in England, and the king and his ministers were able to devote some of their attention to the English colonies in North America. After years of benign neglect, Charles II wanted to reassert his control over what he saw as English territory.

The leaders of Massachusetts Bay Colony were very outspoken in their resistance to royal control. They believed that their charter gave them the right to run their own affairs. At first, Charles II tried to lessen Massachusetts's power by making separate colonies in New Hampshire and Maine. When this failed, the king revoked the charter of Massachusetts Bay Colony in 1684 and made Massachusetts a royal colony.

Firsts in Massachusetts

Massachusetts was the site of many "firsts" in North America:

1621 First Thanksgiving held in Plymouth

1634 First public park: Boston Common

1635 First public school in existence since it was started: Boston Latin School founded

1636 First college: Harvard College founded

1638 First printing press: Stephen Daye established the first printing press in America in Cambridge.

1639 First post office: located in Richard Fairbanks' tavern in Boston; first free school: the Mather School started in Dorchester

1646 First ironworks started in Saugus

1653 First public library: the Boston Public Library

1704 First regularly published newspaper: *Boston Newsletter* established

1716 First lighthouse: Boston Light, built in Boston Harbor

1775 First battle of the American Revolution: the Battle of Lexington and Concord

This building is a reconstruction of the administration building at Saugus, the first iron works in the English colonies, which began operating in 1646. *(Saugus Iron Works National Historic Site [NPS])*

Charles II
(1630–1685)

Charles II was 19 years old when his father was executed in 1649. Charles, his brother James, and many of his father's supporters were forced to leave England. Scotland and parts of Ireland recognized him as king, and in 1651 he invaded England from Scotland with an army of 10,000 men. As Charles made his way south, people turned out to greet his army and proclaim him king. However, on September 3, 1651, Charles's army was defeated by Oliver Cromwell in a battle near the English town of Worcester. Charles fled to France, where he lived in poverty until he returned as king after a royalist army defeated the Puritans. Before he could take the throne, he was forced to give more power to Parliament. Charles II ruled from 1660 until his death in 1685. During his reign, life in England was relatively calm, however, Charles was constantly in need of money to support his lavish lifestyle as king. He may have been trying to make up for the years he had lived in poverty in exile.

Charles II ruled England, Scotland, and Ireland from 1660 until his death in 1685. *(Library of Congress, Prints and Photographs Division [LC-USZ62-96910])*

5

Royal Control

DOMINION OF NEW ENGLAND

After 25 years with Charles II as king, his brother, James II, a Catholic, became king of England in 1685. James's religion created all sorts of problems for him. He was king for only four years before he was overthrown. In that short time, he created havoc in the colonies as well as in England. He did not return Massachusetts Bay Colony's charter. Instead, he consolidated the New England Colonies of Massachusetts, Maine, Plymouth, and Rhode Island into one colony, called the Dominion of New England.

In December 1686, Sir Edmund Andros arrived in Boston to take up his post as royal governor of the Dominion of New England. By 1688 the Dominion of New England had been expanded to include all of New England, Nova Scotia to the north, and New York and New Jersey to the south. Part of the justification for the dominion was the growing conflict between the English colonies and the French colony in Canada. However, Andros ruled the dominion as a dictator backed up by troops he had brought from England.

Andros suspended the colonial governments and set up his own courts. Town meetings were still allowed but could only meet once a year. Andros also levied taxes on the colonies without the consent of the colonists. In addition to the political changes, Andros made changes to the Puritan nature of Massachusetts that angered many. He forced religious toleration on the colony and favored the Church of England over the Puritan churches.

James, Duke of York,
Later King James II
(1633–1701)

In 1649, King Charles I was removed from the throne and executed after a Puritan revolution in England. His two sons, Charles, prince of Wales, and James, duke of York, were forced to spend the next eight years living in exile while the Puritan Oliver Cromwell ran England. Charles lived in poverty in the Netherlands, and James went to Spain, where he joined the Spanish navy in its war against Protestant England. When the English monarchy was restored in 1660, James's older brother became Charles II, king of England.

Charles II appointed James lord high admiral of the navy and in 1664 granted James all the lands between the Connecticut and Delaware Rivers in North America. James sent a fleet to capture the territory claimed by the Dutch and was involved with the fate of New York and New Jersey for the next 24 years.

In 1672, James created a controversy by revealing that he had converted to Catholicism. Although England tolerated many different Protestant sects, the country was not tolerant of Catholics. In fact, in 1673, Parliament passed a series of laws called the Tests Acts, which barred Catholics from holding office. James was forced to resign his position as lord high admiral.

Because his brother had not produced an heir, James was next in line to become king of England. On his brother's death in 1685, many tried to block James from becoming king. However, they were unsuccessful, and he became James II, king of England.

As king, he was faced with a number of uprisings in England. He was extremely brutal in addressing any resistance to his rule. He was so unpopular that, in 1688, he was removed from the throne in a bloodless coup known as the Glorious Revolution. After a brief and unsuccessful attempt to regain his throne, he spent the rest of his life living in exile in France.

James II, shown in an early 19th-century engraving, ruled England for only four years. During that time, he combined Massachusetts, Maine, Plymouth, and Rhode Island to create the Dominion of New England. *(Library of Congress, Prints and Photographs Division [LC-USZ62-92123])*

Dominion of New England, 1686–1689

NEW FRANCE

St. Lawrence R.

Lake
Ontario

Maine
(part of Mass.)

Connecticut R.

Hudson R.

Boston
Massachusetts · Massachusetts
Bay

New York

Connecticut

Plymouth

Rhode Island

Pennsylvania

ATLANTIC
OCEAN

Delaware R.

New York
East Jersey

Philadelphia
West
Jersey

Maryland

Delaware

N

Virginia

	Dominion of New England
	Other British colonies

0   100 miles
0   100 km

The Dominion of New England included New York, New Jersey, Nova Scotia, and all of New England.

When it was learned that James II had been overthrown in a bloodless rebellion referred to as the Glorious Revolution, the colonists seized this as their opportunity to get rid of Andros. Andros had been on a military expedition to the frontier to defend the colonies against raids by Native Americans allied with the French in Canada. When he got back to Boston, the local population was in rebellion. A group had been formed and called itself the "Committee for the Safety of the People." On April 18, 1689, Sir Edmund Andros was arrested and put in Boston's jail by members of the committee. Elsewhere in the dominion, Andros's appointed leaders were also removed from office. Shortly thereafter, Andros and his staff were sent back to England, and the Dominion of New England ended.

In the early days of the American Revolution, many colonists would look back on the overthrow of Edmund Andros as the first act in the long struggle for independence. This may be the case, but the changes affected by enforced religious tolerance and the rule of a royal governor greatly lessened the powers of the Puritan leaders of Massachusetts.

THE ROYAL COLONY OF MASSACHUSETTS

Although the Dominion of New England was dissolved, there were permanent changes that affected Massachusetts. The new rulers of

---

The Importance of New England's Forests

When William and Mary granted a new charter to Massachusetts, there was one clause that may seem a little peculiar to today's readers. England's greatest strength at the time was its navy. As the navy built more ships, it became harder and harder to find trees big enough to use as masts. Therefore, the Massachusetts charter of 1690 reserves all large trees for the navy:

And lastly for the better provideing and furnishing of Masts for Our Royall Navy Wee doe hereby reserve to Vs Our Heires and Successors all Trees of the Diameter of Twenty Four Inches and upwards of Twelve Inches from the ground growing upon any soyle or Tract of Land within Our said Province or Territory not heretofore granted to any private persons And Wee doe restrains and forbid all persons whatsoever from felling cutting or destroying any such Trees.

England, William and Mary, did not restore the original charters to the colonies. Instead, they granted new royal charters. Massachusetts became one royal colony that included the area that would later become the state of Maine. Plymouth Colony became part of Massachusetts. A royal governor was appointed, and the colony was allowed to elect a representative legislature.

As the colony adjusted to its new political situation, war broke out in Europe with England and France as the two major opponents. King William's War, which was waged from 1689 to 1697 in North America, was known as the War of the League of Augsburg in Europe.

In Massachusetts and the other English colonies, warfare was limited to the frontier and was often fought using Native American allies. The Iroquois tribes fought with the English colonists, and the many Algonquian tribes were allied with the French Canadians. For the most part, the war consisted of small raids by both sides.

William Phips was governor of Massachusetts from 1692 to 1694. *(Library of Congress, Prints and Photographs Division [LC-USZ62-110821])*

However, the French governor of Canada, the comte de Frontenac, had bigger plans. He wanted to attack the two major English cities in the Northeast: New York and Boston. Before doing that, French and Native American forces attacked and destroyed three settlements along the frontier: Schenectady, New York; Salmon Falls, New Hampshire; and Fort Loyal, Maine, which was part of Massachusetts at the time. In addition, numerous privateers (privately owned ships licensed to attack others) based in Nova Scotia disrupted trade along the New England coast.

In retaliation for these attacks, the royal governor of Massachusetts, Sir William Phips, raised a force of colonial volunteers and attacked Canada in 1690. The force of 1,300 men in a fleet of 32 ships attacked and captured Port Royal, Nova Scotia. They then went on to attack Quebec. On October 25, 1690, Phips and his fleet gave up and headed home. The fortifications at Quebec City were too much for his small force. The colonists also feared that they might get trapped in the St. Lawrence River by the fast approaching winter.

On the return trip to Boston, the fleet was struck by a series of storms that scattered the ships all along the New England coast and as far away as the Caribbean. In many ways, the expedition was a disaster. Only 30 men died from combat wounds, but almost 500 men died from disease or were lost in shipwrecks. Also, the governor had expected to pay the men out of the goods they captured from the French, so they were not paid. Little was gained in Port Royal, and nothing was captured in Quebec. At the end of the campaign, the government of Massachusetts was £40,000 (pounds, the English currency) in debt. The financial difficulties forced a devaluation, or lowering in value, of the paper money issued by the colony. Also, many towns along the frontier were abandoned out of fear of further attacks.

At this time, the American colonies were generally left alone by England. The merchants and sea captains of Boston expanded their trading during this period. By 1690, there were almost 50,000 people in Massachusetts, which made it second only to Virginia in population. The two largest industries were fishing and shipbuilding. Most of the rest of the population were farmers. The farmers of Massachusetts usually produced a surplus, which the merchants in Boston and the other Massachusetts ports were quick to buy. In addition to trading in fish and farm produce, lumber and other forest products were loaded into the trading vessels that left Massachusetts.

According to the Navigation Acts of 1651, the colonial merchants were supposed to trade only with England and the other English colonies. However, there was not enough business to be done in that limited market, so the ships of Massachusetts were soon carrying goods to ports all around the Atlantic Ocean. With the expansion of trade, rule by a royal governor, and a fast growing population of non-Puritans, the Puritan leaders of Massachusetts were losing control of the colony that had been created to be a model of Puritan beliefs.

It was at about this time that witches started turning up in large numbers in Massachusetts. The witch hysteria of the time

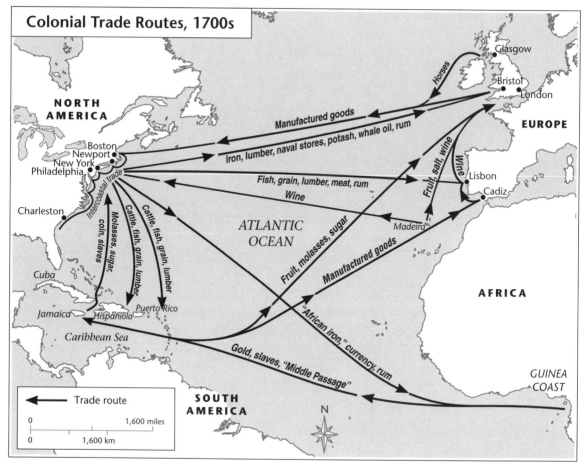

Colonial Trade Routes, 1700s

NORTH AMERICA

EUROPE

Glasgow

Bristol

London

Boston
Newport
New York
Philadelphia

Charleston

Horses

Manufactured goods

Iron, lumber, naval stores, potash, whale oil, rum

Fish, grain, lumber, meat, rum

Wine

Intercoastal trade

Molasses, sugar, coin, slaves

Cattle, fish, grain, lumber

Cattle, fish, grain, lumber

ATLANTIC OCEAN

Fruit, molasses, sugar

Manufactured goods

Fruit, salt, wine

Wine

Lisbon

Cadiz

Madeira

AFRICA

Cuba

Jamaica   Hispaniola   Puerto Rico

Caribbean Sea

"African iron," currency, rum

Gold, slaves, "Middle Passage"

GUINEA COAST

SOUTH AMERICA

N

← Trade route

0   1,600 miles
0   1,600 km

By the time of the Revolution, ships from Massachusetts called at most Atlantic ports in Europe, Africa, South America, and the Caribbean.

created a situation where the focus returned to the religious leaders of the colony. Many have argued that the Puritan ministry eagerly pursued those they thought were witches in an attempt to regain their control of the colony.

6

Witches, Wars, and Awakenings

WITCHES EVERYWHERE

The people of Europe had a long history of believing in and persecuting witches. The English people who came to the colonies brought their beliefs in witchcraft with them. Before 1692, there had been about 60 cases of witchcraft brought before the courts of New England. Of those, less than one-third resulted in convictions, and very few of those convicted were executed. In many of the cases, the accused were older women. The known cases of witchcraft were always a popular topic in the colony. They received the attention of the few newspapers of the time and were often the subject of Sunday sermons by the Puritan ministers.

One case in 1688 resulted in the execution of the widow Glover, an Irish Catholic who lived in Boston. Reverend Cotton Mather, whose father and grandfathers were also important Puritan ministers, preached and wrote about the case. In one of his writings, *Memorable Providences Relating to Witchcraft and Possessions*, he described the case of widow Glover in detail. He went on to warn the people of Massachusetts that they needed to pay more attention to their spiritual lives or the colony could be overtaken by an epidemic of witchcraft.

Governor Phips and Cotton Mather's father, Increase Mather, were key figures in the witch hysteria that swept the colony in

1692. Phips and Increase Mather had gone to England to negotiate a new charter for the colony. When they returned, there were more than 200 people in jail charged with being witches. The governor thought the situation so serious that he called for a special court to try the witches. It was called a Court of Oyer and Terminer, which existed under English law but was used only in extreme situations of social disorder. Some have argued that it was inappropriate in this case.

This engraving illustrates a witchcraft trial in New Haven, Connecticut. The most famous trials occurred in Salem, Massachusetts, and resulted in the execution of 19 people and the deaths of four others due to poor jail conditions. *(Library of Congress, Prints and Photographs Division [LC-USZ6-1299])*

Witchcraft

Most people living in Europe and its colonies in North America in the 17th and 18th centuries believed in witches. The persecution of witches in Europe may have started out as a battle between the growing power of the Catholic Church and the remnants of Europe's pre-Christian religious beliefs. Witchcraft was often associated with the worship of the devil. The Bible talks about the battles between God and Satan for the souls of humankind. Many at the time of the witch hysteria in Massachusetts believed that Satan was actively at work recruiting souls in Massachusetts.

Also, during this time, science had yet to come up with an explanation for many of the diseases and natural disasters that people now understand. Therefore, if a person's house was struck by lightning or a child was born with a disease such as epilepsy, the people of the time might consider it a supernatural act caused by a witch. Medicine was also a science that was little understood, and a person who had learned many folk remedies using plants and other common substances might be suspected of witchcraft.

Added to this in the American colonies were the West African beliefs of Africans who were brought to the colonies and sold as slaves. Their beliefs involved a number of practices that were alien to the Protestant leaders of the colonies. In the islands of the Caribbean, slaves were believed to secretly practice a religion that became known as Voodoo, or Vodun.

Central to the witch hysteria in Massachusetts was Tituba, an enslaved woman who had come to Massachusetts from Barbados and worked in the home of the Salem Village minister, Samuel Parris. Many believe that she shared some of her Voodoo beliefs with Reverend Parris's daughters and niece. Their fear of being charged as witches themselves may have contributed to their strange behavior and accusations against others.

The court was made up of experienced magistrates with the newly appointed deputy governor, William Stoughton, as the chief justice. The biggest problem they faced was that of evidence. The young girls in Salem, who were the main accusers, claimed to have seen the witches in their satanic forms. The girls also frequently had fits in which they claimed they were being tormented by the spectral, or ghostlike, forms of the witches. No one except the girls could see them, and at first the court refused to use the "spectral evidence."

Then, on the insistence of Chief Justice Stoughton, the hysterical ravings of the young girls of Salem were accepted as fact by the court. Those who were willing to confess were spared the gallows, the place where people were hanged. Those who continued to claim innocence were convicted and the executions began. Before public opinion and the officials of the colony brought the hysteria

The Mathers

The most powerful people in Puritan Massachusetts were often the ministers. Winthrop and his followers were interested in creating a Puritan example of the proper way to live and worship. In doing this, the roles of religion and government were often combined. Among the ministers who came with the first migration of Puritans were two who were very important: Richard Mather and John Cotton. Between them, they created a dynasty of religious leaders who would have a great impact on the colony of Massachusetts.

Richard Mather's son, Increase Mather, like many other sons of prominent Puritan leaders, went to Harvard College in Cambridge, Massachusetts. He received his bachelor's degree in 1656. He then earned a master's degree at Trinity College in Dublin, Ireland. Throughout his life, he remained true to the conservative doctrines of the first generation of Puritans.

In 1664, Increase Mather became the minister of the Second Church of Boston, which is now called the Old North Church. For almost 60 years, Increase used his pulpit to try and shape public opinion and political ideals in Massachusetts. He also served as the president of Harvard from 1685 to 1701.

In the 1680s, he was very active in the colony's politics. He went to England in 1688, as the colony's representative, and he tried to get the charter of 1629 restored. While he was in England, the Glorious Revolution took place, and King James II was replaced by King William III. It was called the Glorious Revolution in part because James gave up the throne without any battles being fought.

Unable to get the original charter back, Increase Mather negotiated a new charter for the colony, and he was able to suggest that Sir Williams Phips, a prominent merchant and sea captain from Kittery, Maine (which was then part of Massachusetts), be the colony's first royal governor. Some were disappointed with the new charter, but many understood that Increase Mather had probably gotten the best deal possible considering the situation.

Early in his life, Increase Mather had married John Cotton's daughter, Maria. They named their first son, born in 1663, Cotton Mather in honor of his maternal grandfather. Like both his grandfathers and his father, Cotton Mather became a minister.

Cotton Mather was a brilliant scholar. He graduated from Harvard College at the age of 15. For much of his career as a minister, he shared in the duties of the Second Church with his father. Cotton was a prolific writer. He had almost 400 books, serto an end, 14 women and five men had been hanged as witches. In addition, one man and three women died because of the terrible conditions in the jails.

mons, and other writings published. There were many other writings that had not been published when he died in 1728, just five years after the death of his father.

Like his father, Cotton was also involved in the politics of the day. When word came from England of the Glorious Revolution, he was one of the leaders who was responsible for arresting Governor Edmund Andros and bringing to an end the Dominion of New England.

Both Increase and Cotton Mather were involved in the witch hysteria that struck Salem and many other Massachusetts communities in 1692. Increase worked behind the scenes using his political influence to try and temper the hysteria. He was concerned that the court was accepting too much evidence that could not really be proved.

Cotton, like many in Massachusetts, saw the outbreak of witches as a sign that God was not happy with the way people were living. He believed in witches, as did most people of the time, and thought Satan was truly loose in Massachusetts. One of his most famous books documents that witch hysteria and is titled *Wonders of the Invisible World* (1692).

Cotton Mather did not just write about religious topics. He also had a deep interest in the science of the day. He wrote a number of papers on the flora and fauna (plants and animals) of New England. His writings earned him the honor of being the first person born in North America to be elected to the Royal Society in London in 1713. In many ways, Cotton Mather represented the spirit of Massachusetts. He was obviously a deeply religious man, but he was also interested in all aspects of the world around him: both the natural world and world of men.

A prolific Puritan minister, Cotton Mather believed in witches and played a role in the witchcraft trials held in many Massachusetts communities. *(Library of Congress, Prints and Photographs Division [LC-USZC4-4597])*

Many of the accused who were acquitted were still ruined by the procedure. When they were arrested, their property was seized by the sheriff and was often sold to pay their jail bills. At the time, people in jail were required to pay for their own upkeep as well as for expenses such as transportation to and from jail and court. By the end of September 1692, 156 people from 24 different communities in Massachusetts had been or were being tried for witchcraft. Many more were in jail waiting for their trials.

At this time, Increase Mather and others began to doubt the validity of the whole process. They were especially concerned about the use of "spectral evidence" in court. In January 1693, the governor convened the newly created Massachusetts Superior Court of Judicature, and they took over the witch cases. This court refused to accept "spectral evidence." Without the unseen evidence, the remaining cases were quickly dealt with, and the accused were acquitted. As suddenly as it had started, the witch hysteria was over. However, it would take many families years to recover from the burdens of being falsely accused and imprisoned. Although there were isolated cases of witchcraft in other colonies after 1693, there were no more witch trials in Massachusetts.

Many members of the court publicly apologized four years later. In 1697, the Massachusetts General Court called for a day of forgiveness for those involved, both the accused and the members of the government who had gone after them. The Massachusetts legislature passed a resolution in 1711, which gave financial help to those who had suffered losses because of the trials. Then, in 1714, the legislature officially admitted the innocence of those accused. When the people of Massachusetts finished fighting unseen demons, they were once again faced with conflict with the French and their Native American allies.

QUEEN ANNE'S WAR

The next round of war between England and France started in 1702 and was fought until 1713. The American part of this war is called Queen Anne's War, while in Europe it was known as the War of the Spanish Succession. While war raged in Europe, there was again fighting in the colonies. The southern colonies fought the Spanish in Florida and captured the town of St. Augustine in 1702. However, the Spanish soldiers and townspeople barricaded them-

The Girls Who Cried Witch

In 1689 a new minister came to the church in Salem Village (now Danvers, Massachusetts). Reverend Samuel Parris arrived with his wife, three daughters, his orphaned niece, Abigail Williams, and two servant slaves from the Caribbean, known as Tituba and John Indian. In the winter months of 1692, the Parris's nine-year-old daughter, Elizabeth, and 11-year-old Abigail Williams began to act strangely. The girls were having fits, which included loss of sight and hearing, loss of memory, loss of appetite, choking, and hallucinations where they thought they were being pinched and bitten by demons.

Reverend Parris prescribed fasting and prayer to try and cure the two, but they failed to stop the fits. Parris then took the girls to a number of doctors before Dr. William Griggs diagnosed them as being afflicted by the evil hand of witchcraft. Parris at first denied the possibility that witchcraft could affect his pious family, but many of the people in the community had already come to that conclusion.

It will never be known for sure what happened, but it has been suggested that the girls had been involved in some sort of occult practices with the aid of Tituba and possibly John Indian. Today the symptoms of the two girls would probably be diagnosed as hysteria. It was likely caused by their fear that their occult explorations with Tituba would be found out.

Many believe that the girls then decided to deflect suspicion from themselves by accusing others of witchcraft. Nine other girls in the community also joined the hysteria and made additional accusations. Once the finger pointing began, people who had a grudge against a neighbor accused him or her of witchcraft. Reverend Parris may in fact have contributed to this, as many of the accused in Salem Village were opposed to having him as their minister.

As the trials began, the girls would often have their fits in the courtroom. Afterward, they would testify that one of the accused had come to them in spectral form and tried to attack them. It was this testimony that was responsible for the conviction of many. It was also this testimony that was later ruled inadmissible and put an end to the witch hysteria in Massachusetts.

selves in their stone fort and were able to withstand a long siege. In New England and New York, skirmishes along the border were again frequent. The worst attack by the French and their Native American allies came in 1704.

The frontier of Massachusetts was along the Connecticut River, and there was little settlement between the valley of the Connecticut and the rest of the colony that lived within 30 miles of the

During Queen Anne's War, the French forces allied with Canadian Indians destroyed Deerfield, Massachusetts, on the night of February 29, 1704. The final attack on the town is dramatized in this engraving. *(Library of Congress)*

Atlantic coast. At the northern end of the Connecticut valley was the town of Deerfield, Massachusetts, where about 300 people lived. The French force attacked Deerfield in February 1704, killing 40 people, capturing 111, and burning many of the homes in and around the town. On the forced march north to Canada, another 21 citizens of Deerfield died.

The town's minister, John Williams, was one of the captives, and he later wrote about his experience in *The Redeemed Captive Returning to Zion*. In the book, he wrote about the killing of his wife and two of his children. He also told of the attempts by Catholic priests to convert him and the other prisoners to Catholicism. He and his sons resisted and were eventually allowed to return to Deerfield. His one surviving daughter, Eunice, along with 28 others, decided to stay in Canada. The book was a bestseller at the time and helped to fuel the bad feeling between the English and French colonies.

In the peace treaty signed by France and England at the end of King William's War in 1687, known as the Peace of Ryswick, Port Royal had been given back to the French. During Queen Anne's War, there were two unsuccessful attacks on Port Royal. The governor of Massachusetts, Joseph Dudley, unsuccessfully led the first attack with 1,000 volunteers in 1707. Forces from Massachusetts tried again in 1709 with the same results.

In 1711, 1,500 colonials, many from Massachusetts, joined 11,000 British sailors and soldiers to again attack Quebec City. The British pilots were unfamiliar with the treacherous waters of the St. Lawrence River, and 800 men died in a shipwreck before they

Rangers

From the Pequot War in 1630, and King Philip's War in 1675, through all the wars fought against the French and their Native American allies, the colonists developed into a well-armed population that was trained and ready to fight when necessary. These local soldiers often belonged to militias, which were local groups organized to protect the community on short notice. During the Seven Years' War, as many as 100,000 colonists may have fought at one time or another.

These colonial soldiers were often referred to as "rangers." A ranger was a soldier who operated within a small group and was capable of traveling through the wilderness like his Native American adversaries. During the French and Indian Wars, various groups of rangers were extremely effective in attacking the enemy. These soldiers may not have had the spit and polish of the British regular army troops, but they excelled in the type of warfare that had developed in North America.

By the time of the Revolution, there were numerous soldiers in the colonies who had extensive combat experience. The Americans also had a technological advantage. The British soldiers still carried a smoothbore musket that had limited range. It worked fine in traditional close combat, where the troops lined up on the battlefield and shot repeated volleys at each other. In contrast, the rangers and many militiamen had rifles made in North America that had small grooves in the barrel that would cause the ball they shot to spin. The spin stabilized the ball and made it much more accurate at long distances. The British grossly underestimated the abilities of the colonial militias and paid dearly when their bright red coats became the targets of groups of American rangers.

Joseph Dudley governed Massachusetts and New Hampshire from 1702 until 1715. *(Library of Congress, Prints and Photographs Division [LC-USZ62-120400])*

reached Quebec. At that point, the British commanders decided to withdraw and Quebec once again remained the center of French America.

At the end of Queen Anne's War in 1713, the British made a number of gains in North America. In the settlement of the conflict known as the Peace of Utrecht, the French ceded Acadia (Nova Scotia), Newfoundland, and Hudson's Bay to the English. This really did not mean much to Massachusetts and the other colonies, as there continued to be sporadic raids along the frontier. What did matter was the changing nature of life in the colony. The rule of a royal governor and the expanding importance of trade had profound impacts in Massachusetts.

MERCHANTS AND TRADERS

By the end of Queen Anne's War in 1713, Boston had become the largest community in the colonies. Its superior harbor had made it the commercial center of North America, and its Long Wharf, which extended 2,000 feet into the harbor, was often lined with ships bringing in luxury goods from other ports around the Atlantic Ocean. By this time, the merchants of Massachusetts had found a new product.

The trade with the sugar growers of the Caribbean and South America had created a surplus of molasses. The early Puritans, although they drank beer and hard cider in moderation, were against hard spirits and drunkenness. Being drunk in public was one of the many things a person could end up in the stocks for. However, the merchants of Massachusetts figured they could make a lot more money if they took the molasses and distilled it into rum. By 1717 there were 63 full-time distilleries in Massachusetts. Rum replaced beer and cider as the favorite drink of New Englanders, and barrels of Massachusetts rum filled the holds of many ships.

Some of the rum ended up on the west coast of Africa, where it was traded for Africans to be sold into slavery in the Americas.

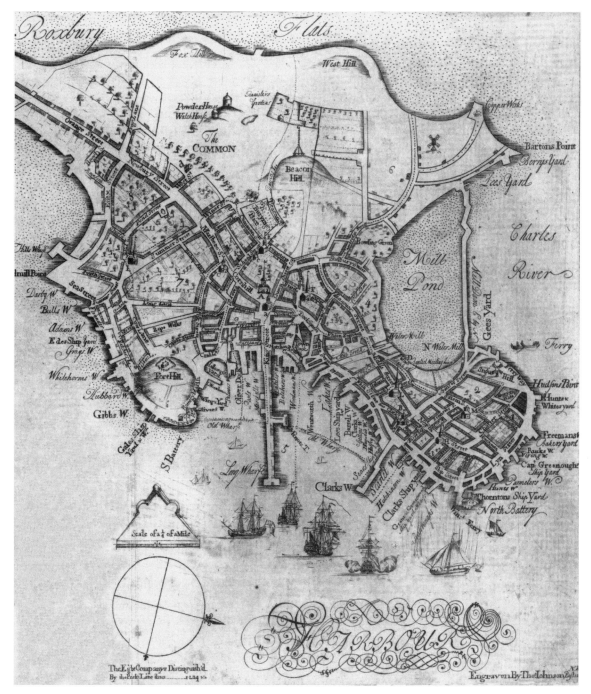

This 1782 map of Boston, founded in 1630, shows the extent of this largest colonial city by the late 18th century. Trade with ports all over the Atlantic Ocean contributed to Boston's development. *(Library of Congress)*

Privateers

During the 17th and 18th centuries, the countries of Europe were at war more than they were at peace. Part of this warfare included attacking the shipping of the other side. Although countries had large navies, there were never enough naval vessels to patrol the entire ocean. To expand their reach, countries would commission privately owned and operated ships to attack their enemies' merchant ships. The commission that a ship owner was given was often referred to as a *letter of marque*. Ships carrying letters of marque were known as privateers. To many, especially those they attacked, they seemed just a notch above pirates who were attacking the merchant ships of the time.

A privateer could legally attack the shipping of a declared enemy and then bring the ship and its cargo into an English port. Once in port, the captured ship and cargo would be turned over to an admiralty court, where its value would be determined. The court would then take a part of the value as payment; the rest of the value of the prizes, as captured ships were called, would be given to the captain and owner of the privateer ship. They would take 40 shares and then give each crew member a single share. Although being given only a single share may not seem fair, a crew member on a successful privateer would earn far more than a regular sailor on a merchant ship would.

The government in England was not the only one enlisting privateers. Colonial governments came to issue letters of marque as well. First these were used to attack the French and their allies during the various French and Indian Wars. Later, the colonial governments and then the Continental Congress used privateers to aid the colonies in their struggle for independence.

Although many in the merchant class had slaves as household servants, slavery was not an important aspect of the Massachusetts economy. Other colonies, primarily in the South, where large plantations growing tobacco, rice, indigo, and sugar predominated, depended on slaves. There were also many more slaves carried in ships from other colonies than by the sea captains of Massachusetts.

While the sea captains brought a taste for foreign goods to the coastal areas of Massachusetts, a gap between life on the coast and life on inland farms grew. But even the small farming communities had strayed away from the ideals of combining the secular (nonreligious) and religious life of the community. Church membership was down throughout the colony in the first quarter of the 18th century, and that was causing great concern for many church leaders. The religious tolerance imposed under the various royal charters since the Dominion of New England had been formed had undermined the powers of the clergy as community leaders. Even Cotton Mather found himself giving communion in Boston's North Church to Anglicans, Baptists, Lutherans, and Presbyterians.

By 1730, there were more than 114,000 people in Massachusetts, and a large segment of the population had come from somewhere other than England. Throughout the colony, there were people who had emigrated from Wales, Scotland, Ireland, Germany, France, and many other European countries. These people came for the opportunity to own land or achieve financial success in some other way. They were not Puritans. They were Catholics, Baptists, Lutherans, and Presbyterians.

Many were disappointed in the loss of religious fervor of the colony, and in 1734 there was a startling reaction. Jonathan Edwards, who had been educated at Yale College in Connecticut, had come upriver to Northampton, Massachusetts, to take over the congregation from his grandfather, Solomon Stoddard. Edwards called for a revival of the original beliefs of the Puritans about salvation and piety.

Soon, people were flocking to his church. By spring 1735, the Northampton church had more than 300 new members, and word of this "Great Awakening," as it is called, spread throughout the colony. But instead of reviving the original ideas of the Puritans, the Great Awakening caused even more divisions in the colony. Many congregations followed the ideas of Edwards and other revivalists, while others continued to worship as they were.

Although the Great Awakening had a large impact on many people in the colony, it did more to point out the fact that Massachusetts had become a place of diversity. People from all over, with varying beliefs, were working together for their own good and the good of the colony as a whole. By this time, many people thought of themselves as citizens of Massachusetts first and then as members of a specific religious group or as citizens of England.

KING GEORGE'S WAR

In 1740 war broke out again between France and England. The European part of the war is called the War of Austrian Succession, while in the North American colonies, where fighting did not break out until 1744, it is known as King George's War. This war, like the two previous ones, was fought primarily along the frontier where the English settlements were in constant danger of attack by the French and their Native American allies. Over the years, Massachusetts had built a number of forts in the Connecticut River Valley, which served to protect the settlements there. They had also built forts farther up the river in New Hampshire, which caused some conflict with the neighboring colony. In the end, New Hampshire made it clear that the forts were located on their lands. However, since they primarily served to protect the settlements downriver in Massachusetts, it was decided that Massachusetts could continue to garrison and support the forts.

After the last war, England had gained control of Nova Scotia, but the French had kept the large island of Cape Breton just to the northeast of the mainland. At Louisbourg on Cape Breton, the French proceeded to fortify the harbor with a huge fort and outlying artillery batteries. Louisbourg was to serve in the dual role as a safe harbor for French shipping and as a protector of the entrance to the St. Lawrence River. When fighting broke out, the French at Louisbourg decided to attack Nova Scotia. They easily captured the fishing village of Canso. In fact, when confronted by the large French force, the small garrison negotiated for their surrender. The major concession they wanted was to be transported to Boston instead of becoming French prisoners. The French agreed but took them to Louisbourg first.

When the prisoners finally arrived in Boston, the people of Massachusetts were extremely upset by their reports of French aggression. The Massachusetts governor, William Shirley, called a secret session of the Massachusetts assembly and proposed an attack on Louisbourg using the intelligence gathered from the recently arrived

Depicted here in an engraving, William Shirley served as governor of Massachusetts from 1741 to 1756.
(Library of Congress, Prints and Photographs Division [LC-USZ62-85100])

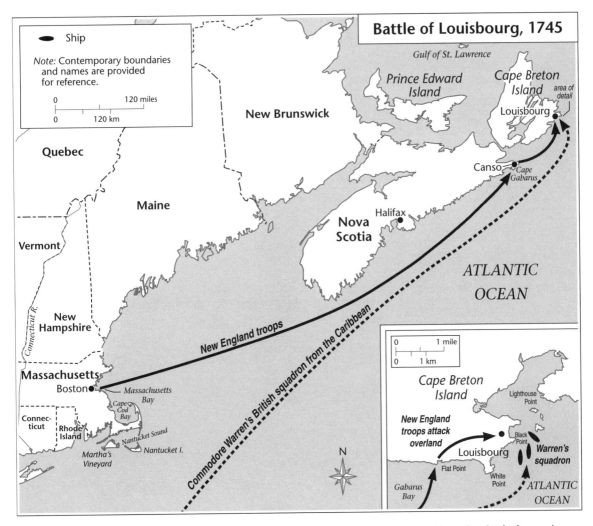

Battle of Louisbourg, 1745

Troops from New England and a British naval squadron rendezvoused in Canso, Nova Scotia, before going on to attack the French fortress at Louisbourg. The British ships blockaded the harbor while 4,000 troops from New England landed and attacked the fort from its poorly defended landside.

captives. At first, Shirley's plan was rejected. However, when news leaked out that the legislature had denied Shirley's plan, there was such an uproar in Boston that the legislature reconsidered, and plans were made to attack Louisbourg.

Governor Shirley wrote to England requesting help from the English fleet in the Caribbean that was commanded by Commodore Peter Warren. In spring 1745, a force was assembled. It

Under the command of William Pepperrell, a volunteer militia with members from Massachusetts, Connecticut, and New Hampshire defeated the French at Louisbourg, Cape Breton Island. *(Library of Congress, Prints and Photographs Division [LC-USZ62-105732])*

consisted of 3,000 volunteer militia from Massachusetts, 500 from Connecticut, and 450 from New Hampshire. Other colonies provided supplies, ships, and cannons for the expedition. As com-

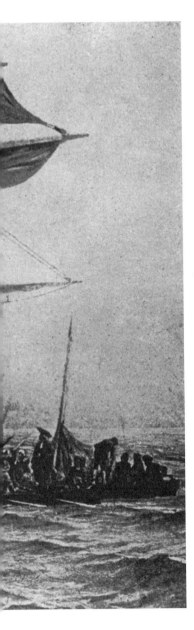

mander, Shirley selected William Pepperrell, who was the president of the Massachusetts legislature, a colonel in the militia, and a successful merchant from Kittery in the district of Maine.

When Pepperrell left Boston, he had 4,000 militia under his command, 15 armed ships, and more than 100 transports. The forces were to meet in Canso before attacking Louisbourg. On April 23, Commodore Warren sailed into Canso in command of a 60-gun-ship, with two 40-gun ships as part of his squadron. On the 29th, they all sailed the short distance to Louisbourg. However, they did not attack directly. Instead, they entered the large bay to the southwest of the fortress and out of range of its guns.

It would have been foolish to attack the fort directly. Instead, Pepperrell landed his forces and then moved around behind the town where they could bombard it. The fortifications had been designed to protect the harbor, and the fort's big guns could not be swung around to fire on the colonial militia. With the colonials attacking from the rear and Warren preventing any ships from entering or leaving the harbor, the undermanned and sickly garrison eventually surrendered. The greatest fortress in North America was captured, with just over 100 deaths for the colonials.

When word reached Boston of the victory, many celebrations were held. Warren was promoted to admiral. Pepperrell was made a baronet by the king: the first person born in North America to receive such a distinction. In honor of the battle, a square on Boston's Beacon Hill was named Louisbourg Square, and it is still surrounded by some of Boston's finest old houses. The victory at Louisbourg was seen by many as an example of the growing power of the colonies, especially in Massachusetts.

However, the campaign was not without its problems. Many men were left behind to maintain the fortress and hold it against the French, but by spring 1746, almost 900 of them had died of disease. The French mounted two attempts to recapture Louisbourg but never fired a shot. The first fleet was sent back to France by a series of storms in the Atlantic Ocean. The second fleet was ravaged by an epidemic before it encountered a British fleet and was defeated.

The Battle of Louisbourg was a victory that many in the colonies were very proud of. They had done their part to help secure their corner of the world. They also had done service to the cause of England. It was with much dismay and anger that the people of Massachusetts and the other colonies that had lent support greeted the news of the Treaty of Aix-la-Chapelle. In the treaty, which ended King George's War, the English traded Louisbourg back to the French for control of the colony of Madras in India. The king agreed to reimburse Massachusetts for the cost of capturing Louisbourg, which only partly soothed the colonials' anger. Despite peace in Europe, fighting continued along the frontier as both the English and French colonies tried to expand their borders. It would be these border conflicts that would once again throw France and England into war.

THE SEVEN YEARS' WAR

The first three French and Indian wars had all started in Europe and then spilled over to the French and English colonies. The final conflict between France and England in North America is known as the Seven Years' War. It started in North America and then spread to all the corners of the world where France and England had colonies, as well as to Europe. The war started in 1754 in the Ohio River Valley, where the French came in conflict with English colonists from Virginia and Pennsylvania.

Unlike the previous conflicts, large numbers of British regular troops were sent to the colonies to attack the French and finally settle the question of who would control North America. Many members of the colonial militia fought with the regular army. Massachusetts did its share by providing militia that fought in upstate New York and in Canada when both Quebec and Montreal were captured. In addition, a number of colonial ships were hired as transport for the British forces, while other ship captains were given letters of marque, which gave them a legal right to attack enemy shipping.

A ship that was operating under a letter of marque was referred to as a privateer. When the colonies began the War for

The Massachusetts militia aided the British in many upstate New York battles during the Seven Years' War. In this particular engraving, General Louis-Joseph de Montcalm tries to prevent American Indians from attacking British soldiers as they leave Fort William Henry. *(Library of Congress, Prints and Photographs Division [LC-USZ62-120704])*

Independence, privateers were the only naval force they had. Many Massachusetts ships were involved in the Seven Years' War, and many merchants added substantially to their fortunes by supplying the British forces. Many colonial soldiers gained experience during this war that would be of great value when it came time to fight for independence just 12 years after the end of the war.

When the Treaty of Paris was signed in 1763, France gave up its claims in North America, with the exception of two small islands at the mouth of the St. Lawrence River. The islands of St. Pierre and Miquelon remain French territory today. Britain now controlled all the continent of North America east of the Mississippi, with the exception of New Orleans and a poorly defined stretch of land along the Gulf coast referred to as northwest Florida, which belonged to the Spanish. These two exceptions and everything to the west of the Mississippi would belong to Spain, at least for a while.

Although no battles were fought in Massachusetts during the Seven Years' War, the impact on the colony was immense. Despite the profits made by merchants during the war, many in the colony had come to resent the presence of British troops in North America. Even though Massachusetts and the other colonies involved

Albany Plan

When seven colonies sent representatives to Albany, New York, in 1754, one of their most pressing topics was defending the colonies against the French and their Native American allies. Governor William Shirley of Massachusetts and Benjamin Franklin worked together to come up with a plan of defense. What they suggested is known as the Albany Plan. It called for colonial defenses to be put under the control of one chief military executive and for there to be one commissioner for Indian affairs for all the colonies.

In addition, the plan had provisions for a grand council of delegates that would have representatives from all thirteen colonies. The Albany Plan was taken back to the seven colonies that had sent representatives. Not one colonial legislature agreed to the plan. In 1754, there was too much competition between the colonies for them to unite in their common defense. Over the next 20 years, that would change dramatically.

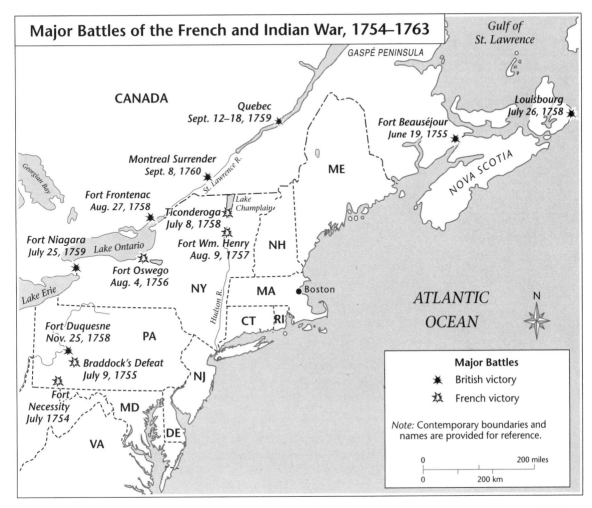

Major Battles of the French and Indian War, 1754–1763

Gulf of
St. Lawrence

GASPÉ PENINSULA

CANADA

Quebec
Sept. 12–18, 1759

Fort Beauséjour
June 19, 1755

Louisbourg
July 26, 1758

Montreal Surrender
Sept. 8, 1760

St. Lawrence R.

ME

NOVA SCOTIA

Georgian Bay

Fort Frontenac
Aug. 27, 1758

Ticonderoga
July 8, 1758

Lake
Champlain

Fort Niagara
July 25, 1759

Lake Ontario

Fort Wm. Henry
Aug. 9, 1757

NH

Fort Oswego
Aug. 4, 1756

Lake Erie

NY

Hudson R.

MA

Boston

ATLANTIC
OCEAN

N

Fort Duquesne
Nov. 25, 1758

PA

CT

RI

Braddock's Defeat
July 9, 1755

NJ

Fort
Necessity
July 1754

MD

DE

VA

Major Battles

★ British victory

✷ French victory

Note: Contemporary boundaries and
names are provided for reference.

0   200 miles
0   200 km

During the Seven Years' War, militia from Massachusetts took part in the capture of two major French cities, Quebec and Montreal.

had not agreed to form a single colonial authority at the Albany Congress in 1754, there was a growing sentiment that the colonies could take care of themselves.

Ideas about the colonies were also changing in England. The Seven Years' War had doubled the country's national debt, and many thought that it was time for the colonies to pay their share. Up until this point, the English kings and their advisers had allowed the colonies to operate with very little control from London. Only a very few taxes were enacted, and many of those were not enforced. The results had been a huge growth in commerce

This *half-house,* or "half–Cape Cod," known as the Rowell House and located in Barnstable County, Massachusetts, was built around 1730. This distinctive American home, a one-room cottage, is the smallest type of Cape Cod home traditionally built. *(Library of Congress, Prints and Photographs Division, HABS [HABS, MASS, 1-WEL, 14-2])*

between the colonies and Great Britain. Merchants on both sides of the Atlantic had become wealthy because of the freewheeling and often illegal trade in the colonies.

The attempts to enforce existing trade laws, such as the Molasses Act of 1733, and the passing of numerous new laws and taxes contributed greatly to the independence movement in Massachusetts. Many of the leaders of the independence movement came from the merchants and traders who were hit hardest by Britain's attempts to collect what they felt they were owed.

After the Treaty of Paris, France continued to cause problems as well. The French encouraged trade with the English colonies, although it was illegal in the eyes of the British. When the Revolution came, the French were eager to take the side of the colonies in retribution for their own losses in North America at the hands of the British.

By 1760, there were more than 220,000 people in Massachusetts and more than 1.5 million in the thirteen English colonies combined. Very few of these people had been born in England. Many were native-born Americans living in homes that were uniquely American. Many others had emigrated from other countries in Europe. So it is not surprising that the colonies would resent the change in British attitude after the Treaty of Paris.

7

The Road to Revolution

THE SUGAR ACT

The Molasses Act of 1733 was designed to force the merchants in Massachusetts and other colonies to buy their molasses only from the English colonies in the Caribbean. The act placed a tax of six pence a gallon on molasses that did not come from other English colonies. The tax was so high that it was ignored by most traders who continued to import molasses, especially from the French islands in the Caribbean even during the Seven Years' War.

Molasses was smuggled into many ports in Massachusetts. Even when someone was caught smuggling molasses or other goods, they were almost never convicted. The British-appointed customs agents had to bring their cases before local courts, and there was not a jury in Massachusetts that would convict a fellow colonist in an alleged crime against the Crown. The rum trade affected almost everyone in the colony.

Farmers were still supplying the plantations of the Caribbean with food and animals. In addition, hundreds of people worked in the many distilleries that produced rum. Many others worked in the industries that provided the ships and materials needed to outfit and maintain them. Rope making, sail making, lumber mills, iron works, and numerous other businesses were profiting from the large amount of trade done by the merchants and ship owners of Massachusetts. It seemed only natural that someone working in

James Otis
(1725–1783)

James Otis became an important leader of the resistance to the Crown when he defended some of the Boston merchants in 1761 who were accused of possessing goods that had been smuggled into the colony. In court he declared that the American colonists had certain natural rights that the laws of Parliament could not overrule. Otis's declaration of these natural rights would become one of the underlying themes of the problems between Britain and its American colonies.

James Otis defended the colonists' right to rule themselves without interference by the British. *(Library of Congress, Prints and Photographs Division [LC-USZ62-102561])*

one of these businesses would be reluctant to convict a ship captain or a merchant for bringing in the molasses that was so important to the colony's economy.

After the Treaty of Paris in 1763, George Grenville became the chief minister of the British government. He knew that the government had to increase its revenues to pay for the war that had just ended. He also thought it was time for the colonies to pay their share. To do this, Grenville came up with a new way to tax sugar and molasses. Rather than have a very high tax on foreign molasses as the 1733 act did, he proposed a much lower tax on sugar and molasses imported into the colonies.

This new law was called the Sugar Act of 1764. At first, it appeared that this was a good thing for the merchants and distillers of Massachusetts. However, in addition to lowering the tax, the Sugar Act changed and strengthened the situation for the customs agents whose job it was to collect the tax.

The Sugar Act took the prosecution of smugglers out of the hands of the lenient local courts and juries and gave authority to a new naval court set up in Halifax, Nova Scotia. This court, called a Vice Admiralty Court, was run by people appointed by the king, and there were no juries involved. So, instead of having a high tax that was never collected, everyone involved in the rum trade was now forced to pay taxes.

Although a number of Massachusetts merchants got together to complain officially about the new tax situation, their protests were primarily about the economic impact of the Sugar Act. For most people in the colony, the Sugar Act had little direct impact. However, the Stamp Act would be a different story.

THE STAMP ACT

The Sugar Act did not produce the revenue that Grenville had wanted. It was costing over £200,000 a year to keep a military force in North America to defend the colonies. Grenville felt the colonies should pay half and then Parliament would pay the other half. To come closer to achieving that goal, Grenville proposed a stamp tax for the colonies.

A stamp tax requires that an actual stamp be purchased and placed on certain goods before they can be sold. It is a practice that was long established in England, and it is still used in the United States. Not that long ago, every pack of cigarettes and bottle of alcohol sold had a tax stamp on it. People in the United States still pay those same taxes today, although stamps are no longer used.

Grenville's Stamp Act affected almost everyone in every colony. Most business transactions that had to be recorded required that it be done on a stamped piece of paper. This included land transactions, all sorts of licenses, the documents that a ship needed to export or import goods, and documents drawn up by a lawyer— all needed a stamp. In addition, every newspaper, pamphlet, and advertisement circulated in the colonies required a stamp, as did consumer items like cards and dice. Whereas the Sugar Act had only directly affected a few, the Stamp Act would be paid by almost everyone.

The reaction to the Sugar Act had been a few wealthy merchants getting together and writing letters. The Stamp Act created a much wider and immediate reaction. When the people of Boston heard about the Stamp Act and the taxes they would be paying because of it, they took to the streets. This time the reaction was not just about the cost. The people of Massachusetts and a number of the other colonies saw the Stamp Act as an infringement on their rights.

They felt that the English Parliament did not have the right to tax them, because they were not represented in Parliament. In England, government officials felt that the Parliament represented all English subjects, whether they could vote or not. The protests in Massachusetts came at all levels.

In Braintree, Massachusetts, John Adams, who would become a leader of the Revolution and the (second) president of the United States, wrote a document that became known as the Braintree Instructions. It expressed the feeling of the town meeting that the Stamp Act was wrong for many reasons. The Instructions were intended for the representatives of Braintree in the Massachusetts legislature. Adams wrote that the Stamp Act would be a financial burden on the people of the colony. But even more important, Adams wrote, "no Freeman should be subjected to any Tax to which he has not given his own consent in person or by proxy." This sentiment would be later stated simply as "no taxation without representation."

The thoughts expressed in Adams's Braintree Instructions were so widely held that more than 40 towns in Massachusetts followed with similar documents within the next few months. And this all happened before a single stamp had arrived in the colonies.

When affixed to goods, this stamp signified that a tax must be paid upon purchase. Many colonists felt that the British unfairly introduced these taxes when they implemented the Stamp Act in 1765, which affected goods ranging from business transactions to playing cards. *(Library of Congress, Prints and Photographs Division [LC-USZ61-539])*

Andrew Oliver was to be the person in Boston in charge of distributing the stamps. On August 14, 1765, a mob marched through the streets of Boston carrying an effigy of Oliver with a noose around its neck and then tore down a building he had built on the waterfront. Less then two weeks later, another mob attacked the house of the lieutenant governor, Thomas Hutchinson.

Hutchinson, although a member of a long-established Boston family, like many, took the side of England on most issues and had been rewarded with a number of political appointments in the colony. In the years between the Stamp Act and the Revolution, Hutchinson was often on the side of the Crown against those in Massachusetts who considered themselves patriots.

By the time the Stamp Act went into effect on November 1, 1765, there had been so much strong opposition that it was never really implemented. The people who were supposed to distribute the stamps feared if they did, they would have to face the mobs. Those who were supposed to buy the stamps were convinced they could continue to conduct their business without them. The anti-British sentiment had grown to the point where merchants were beginning to have trouble selling goods that had been imported from England.

It was the Stamp Act that also brought about groups that were organized to direct the actions of the mobs. In Boston this group was first called the Loyal Nine. They later adopted the name that was used in other colonies by similar groups—The Sons of Liberty. John Hancock, John Adams, Samuel Adams, and other influential men in the colony were leaders of the Sons of Liberty.

On an official level, the Massachusetts legislature sent a letter to the other colonial legislatures calling for a meeting to discuss the Stamp Act. In October, 1765, 27 delegates from nine colonies gathered in New York City. They drafted a protest of the Stamp Act and earlier Sugar Act. They said that it was the "undoubted right of Englishmen, that no Taxes be imposed on them, but with their own Consent, given personally or by their Representatives."

While the colonies were experiencing all the protests of the Stamp Act, things were not going well for its major supporter, James Grenville. King George III had never been pleased with Grenville and forced him out of office in summer 1765. The person who replaced him, Lord Charles Rockingham, had opposed

Samuel Adams
(1722–1803)

Samuel Adams may have been the most important leader of the revolutionary movement in Massachusetts. Although unsuccessful in business, losing both a newspaper and a brewing business, he was someone the people of Boston willingly followed, and he had a very active political career. He was one of the founders of the Loyal Nine, a secret group that worked to reverse the tyranny of the Crown. This group became the Sons of Liberty and, with Adams as the leader, played a major role in inciting the Boston Massacre and implementing the action known as the Boston Tea Party.

Throughout the pre-Revolutionary struggles with England, Adams was also in the lead. He was responsible for the creation of the Committee of Correspondence and as chair of the Boston Town Meeting contributed greatly to the anti-British writings that were distributed through the committees. He also served in the Continental Congress. Later in life, he stayed in Massachusetts and served in state politics. With his longtime friend and fellow patriot John Hancock, he was in part responsible for Massachusetts ratifying the U.S. Constitution in 1788.

Samuel Adams has been overlooked by many historians, in part because his career after the Revolution did not rise to the national level, like his relative John Adams and other early American presidents: Washington, Jefferson, and Madison. His signature was not as large and flamboyant as Hancock's, but it is there on the Declaration of Independence. And that document reflects what he wrote for the Boston Committee of Correspondence about people's natural rights of life, liberty, and property, and the responsibility of the people to defend their rights in an article entitled "The Rights of Colonists."

Samuel Adams was integral in the move to demand independence from England.
(Library of Congress, Prints and Photographs Division [LC-D416-256])

the Stamp Act from the beginning. The Stamp Act was repealed on March 18, 1767, without ever really being put into effect.

Although many in the colonies thought they had won a major victory, Rockingham had Parliament pass the Declaratory Act in 1766. This act made it clear that Parliament was well within its rights to pass any laws it saw fit for any part of the British Empire, including the colonies in North America. Boston would learn just how serious the government in London was about asserting control of the colonies when troops were sent to protect the customs agents in Boston and the resulting Boston Massacre in 1770.

THE BOSTON MASSACRE

At the same time as the Declaratory Act was passed in 1767, another law was passed by Parliament. This was the Quartering Act passed in 1768, which stated that the colonies would be responsible for providing for the housing and feeding of British troops stationed in the colonies. At first, this seemed like a reasonable law. However, it was mistakenly assumed that British troops in the colonies would be there to defend the people, not be used against them.

King George III's government was still losing money on the colonies and needed to find a way to raise money without causing more riots. Benjamin Franklin of Pennsylvania had been in London during the debate over taxing the colonies and had said that direct taxes, like the Stamp Act, imposed on the colonies were wrong. He went on to say that a duty (a tax on imports and exports) that was intended for the entire British Empire would be acceptable.

One of the government leaders in London, Charles Townshend, proposed that Parliament enact a number of duties on items that had to be imported by the colonies. These included painter's color, lead, glass, paper, and tea. The Townshend Duties, enacted in 1767, did not bring about the type of reaction that the Stamp Act had had in Massachusetts. However, the customs agents were still having a very hard time collecting money and stopping smuggling into major trading ports such as Boston and New York.

To assist the customs agents, troops were sent in. Seven hundred "redcoats" were sent to Boston. The British army soldiers of the time were called redcoats because of the color of their uniforms. At first there was an attempt made to house the troops in private homes. This was resisted with such vigor that the officials decided to house the troops in some vacant buildings in Boston.

Although they were not living in the homes of Boston, the red-coats and the people of the community came in contact regularly. There were numerous reports of fights between off-duty soldiers and local citizens. Many in Boston, and in the surrounding communities, were very upset that the soldiers were there. They saw them for what they were—a force sent to impose the Crown's will on the people of Massachusetts.

On March 5, 1770, the simmering tension between the people of Boston and the redcoats boiled over. The incident started when a British soldier guarding the Customs House was verbally attacked by a young man. The soldier hit the man in the head with the butt of his rifle, and the man ran off yelling for help. The alarm was sounded. Someone even began ringing the bells in one of the

Paul Revere's engraving of the Boston Massacre depicts the event that many consider the beginning of the struggle for independence. It occurred on March 5, 1770. *(Library of Congress, Prints and Photographs Division [LC-USZ62-35522])*

nearby churches. Soon a large and angry crowd had gathered at the Customs House.

It has been estimated that around 400 Bostonians were in the mob. The sentry had also sent for reinforcements, and Captain Thomas Preston and six soldiers responded, as well as other soldiers who were in the building. The crowd began throwing snowballs and chunks of ice at the soldiers. When the crowd refused to disperse, Preston gave the order for his men to load their weapons. No one has ever learned who gave the order, but someone yelled "Fire!" and the six soldiers in the street and four more in the Customs House fired their rifles into the mob. Three men died there in the street, and two others died shortly after from their wounds. One of the first to fall was Crispus Attucks, who was one of the mob's leaders. Attucks was half Native American and half African American. He and the other four who died were considered by many as the first casualties in the struggle for independence.

As a result of the Boston Massacre, all British troops were pulled out of Boston, and Captain Preston and 10 soldiers were arrested. At the trial that took place in fall 1770, John Adams and Josiah Quincy were the defense attorneys for the soldiers. Despite the fact that both lawyers were part of the anti-British movement in the colony, they took the case to see that justice was done. The local press tried to show the soldiers as brutal murderers. However, the facts did not support the claims. In the end, Preston and eight of the soldiers were acquitted. Two soldiers were convicted of manslaughter. Because of an old law that allowed clergy (and that had come to be applied to anyone who could read) to be excused from prison in manslaughter cases, the two soldiers were branded on their hands and then returned to the army.

With the troops gone and the colony experiencing a period of prosperity, it seemed that the situation was under control. All the Townshend Duties, except the one on tea, were repealed. However, for those who decided the only path for Massachusetts was independence, the Boston Massacre would remain an important example of British tyranny.

THE BOSTON TEA PARTY

During the next few years, it seemed that the conflict between the colony of Massachusetts and the king's government had lessened.

However, behind the scenes, those interested in more rights or even independence for the people of the colonies were still very active. The people in favor of colonial rights and independence are referred to as Whigs, while the governor and those loyal to the government in England were called Loyalists.

To counteract the Whigs, the royal governor of Massachusetts, Thomas Hutchinson, made sure that only Loyalists were given jobs in the government. At the same time, rules were changed by Parliament to have both the governor and judges in the colonies paid directly from London. Although these people were appointed by the king or his representative, in the past they had been paid by the colonial legislatures. This was seen by many as an attempt to clarify exactly whom officials in the colonies were responsible to.

Many Whigs saw this as a very dangerous precedent. They felt the government should serve the people and therefore should be

Crispus Attucks and Slavery in Massachusetts

Crispus Attucks had been born a slave. In Massachusetts, slaves were fairly common and primarily used as household servants. During various conflicts with Native Americans, captives were often taken and sold into slavery. There were also a number of African-American slaves in Massachusetts. Attucks is believed to have been the child of a Native American and an African-American slave.

Although there were slaves in the colony, and some of the Massachusetts ships participated in the slave trade, in colonial Massachusetts African Americans were never more than 1 or 2 percent of the total population. The population of Massachusetts in 1760 is estimated to have been more than 220,000 people. Of those, fewer than 5,000 were of African-American descent. In comparison, Virginia at the time was 41 percent African American, and South Carolina was 60 percent African American.

Crispus Attucks had run away from the people who held him as a slave in 1750, when he was 27 years old. He spent the next 20 years working as a seaman on numerous ships sailing out of Boston. Attucks, it is assumed, understood the importance of freedom, and that is why he was at the front of the mob waving a club at the soldiers. It has been reported that more than 10,000 people participated in the procession that took his casket to its place of burial in the Granary Burying Ground in Boston. More than a hundred years later, the city of Boston erected a monument to the five men who died in the Boston Massacre. It is called the Crispus Attucks Monument.

paid by the people's representatives in the legislature. As Hutchinson's grip on the government tightened, Samuel (Sam) Adams, a member of the legislature, and others in Boston saw a need for the people of Massachusetts to have a way to express and share their ideas about their government. A system of sharing information between the colonies had already been established. The system was called a committee of correspondence, and people in each colonial legislature were responsible for corresponding with the committee members in the other colonial legislatures. This way the colonial legislatures were kept aware of what was going on throughout the colonies.

Sam Adams saw this as a method for the communities of Massachusetts to communicate their ideas about government with each other. Toward the end of 1772, Sam Adams and the members of the Boston town meeting agreed to set up a Committee of Correspondence and to invite all the communities of Massachusetts to do the same. As a starting point, the Boston Committee of Correspondence sent out a pamphlet to each town that contained its views about the rights of people in the colony.

This document became known as the Boston Pamphlet, and it was well received in the towns. In fact, the response from many of the towns was more radical than the position taken by the Boston committee. Governor Hutchinson was extremely alarmed by the favorable response the Boston Pam-

Shown here is Faneuil Hall, a town-meeting place in Boston. At this location in 1772, Samuel Adams suggested that the colonies unite against England. *(National Archives, Still Picture Records, NWDNS-208-PR-10D-1)*

phlet received. The relative quiet of the previous two years had lulled him into a false sense of security.

Hutchinson felt he needed to respond. On January 6, 1773, he called the legislature into session and made what he thought would be a very convincing speech that would return the people of Massachusetts to the path of loyalty to King George III and England. After a long and very carefully constructed speech that defended the role of the king and Parliament to rule the colonies as they saw fit, Hutchinson concluded by stating that the people of Massachusetts had to make a choice. He said, "I know of no line that can be drawn between the supreme authority of Parliament and the total independence of the colonies."

Hutchinson was trying to say that there was no middle ground and that people had either to respect the Crown's authority or seek independence from it. He said this assuming that his audience would never consider the second choice and would have to come to the conclusion that loyalty was their only path.

The Whigs in the audience that day were stunned to silence. Many of them thought the colonies should work toward independence, but they had not yet openly advocated it. For the king's governor to force the issue shocked many. Soon Hutchinson realized he had made a huge blunder. Instead of winning the Whigs to his point of view, he had forced the call for independence.

Within the year, it became clear to many that independence was the only answer. Up until this point, resistance and protest had been loosely organized and local. Now the Sons of Liberty were becoming a force to be reckoned with in Massachusetts and other colonies. When the English Parliament passed the Tea Act in 1773, to bail out the failing East India Company, they unknowingly started the chain of events that would lead to the War for Independence.

Many had called for independence, but few before this time thought it would come as a result of a war with Britain, which at the time was the 18th-century equivalent of a "superpower" today. Most of the tea consumed in the colonies at the time was smuggled in via trade with the Dutch. The Tea Act required the colonies to buy English tea. Once again, Parliament had underestimated the colonial reaction.

In some colonies, the protests were so strong that the English tea was never landed. In other places, the people appointed to be the "tea agents" quit rather than face the anger of their neighbors. In Boston, however, Governor Hutchinson still had enough control that the ships came into port with 90,000 pounds of tea worth

£10,000. On December 16, 1773, under the cover of darkness, a group of as many as 60 men, disguised as Native Americans, boarded the three ships—the *Dartmouth, Beaver,* and *Eleanor.* They then dumped 340 cases of tea into the harbor. No damage was done to the ships, and no one was injured. Even a padlock that had been broken to get into the hold of one of the ships was replaced.

The message of the Boston Tea Party, as it was called, was startlingly clear to all: The colonies were willing to go to great lengths to prevent Parliament from dictating to them. Throughout all the colonies, a successful boycott of English tea followed. There were even other "tea parties" in other colonies. It seemed to the members of Parliament that this was a time for strong action.

To punish the people of Boston, in 1774 Parliament passed the Coercive Acts, also known in the colonies as the Intolerable Acts. The two parts of the acts that caused the most alarm were known as the Boston Port Bill, passed on March 31, 1774, and the Massachusetts Government Act, passed on May 20, 1774. The Port Bill closed the port of Boston until the community paid for the tea that had been dumped into the harbor. Closing the port had an immediate impact: People were thrown out of work, food became scarce, and

To protest the passage of the Tea Act, some male colonists, disguised as American Indians, boarded three ships in Boston Harbor on December 16, 1773, and dumped hundreds of cases of tea into the harbor. The event became known as the Boston Tea Party. *(Library of Congress)*

many businesses were forced to close. The Massachusetts Government Act made major changes in the colony's charter. It took power away from elected officials and returned it to the Crown.

Although not directly affected, many people in other colonies were extremely concerned about the treatment of the people of Massachusetts. They realized that Parliament and the king felt they could do as they pleased with the colonies. Many had thought that they were protected by their charters, and now they saw that was not true. Throughout the colonies, people followed Massachusetts's lead and formed committees of correspondence. They also organized relief efforts to send food and other needed goods overland to Boston and the rest of Massachusetts.

Throughout Massachusetts and in other colonies, the local militias, which had been relatively inactive since the end of the Seven Years' War, reorganized and began drilling. The plan was to have the militia ready at a minute's notice if they were needed. Because of this, the local militia in many places became known as minutemen. As minutemen drilled and the Committees of Correspondence wrote back and forth, it became apparent that the colonies would have to plan a united response to the Intolerable Acts.

The Suffolk Resolves

Boston and the surrounding towns make up Suffolk County, and when it became obvious that the Crown was intent on controlling the state legislature, each county in Massachusetts held a convention so they could agree on a course of action. Under the leadership of Sam Adams, the Suffolk County convention drew up its position.

Joseph Warren took on the task of writing out the convention's ideas. In what became known as the Suffolk Resolves, British soldiers in Boston were labeled "military executioners" and the Coercive Acts were called "murderous." There were also strong words used against King George III and his chief minister, Lord Frederick North.

The Resolves went on to plot a course of action for Massachusetts and, after the Continental Congress adopted them, all the colonies. They suggested that tax collectors not send any money collected to England, that the colonial councilors appoint new governors, and that people ignore the rulings of judges appointed by the Crown. At this point, there was no call for war or independence.

The call went out from Massachusetts asking each colony to send representatives to a meeting in Philadelphia, Pennsylvania, in September 1774. This meeting is called the First Continental Congress, and the representatives passed three resolutions. The first was the adoption of the Suffolk Resolves on September 17. This was a response to the Intolerable Acts by the county convention in Suffolk County, Massachusetts.

The county conventions and the Continental Congress made it clear that there was intense anger over the Intolerable Acts. However, the opportunity still existed for the Crown to reach a compromise with the colonies. Most would have welcomed a situation where the colonies were granted more control over their own destinies while still remaining a part of the British Empire. King George III and Lord North wanted nothing to do with compromise, and it was their actions in Massachusetts that sent the two sides to war.

8

The War of
Independence

When England passed the Coercive Acts in 1774, the king appointed a new governor for Massachusetts who would be in charge of enforcing the acts and getting control of the colony. General Thomas Gage was the commander of the British armed forces in North America, and he became governor of Massachusetts as well. The king and his councilors felt that a show of force was all that was needed to bring the colony in line. They continued to believe this, even after war had broken out between England and the colonies. They sent enough naval ships to blockade Boston Harbor and 3,000 soldiers to subdue the dissidents in the colony.

Gage felt this was far too few soldiers to go against the huge number of minutemen in Massachusetts. He knew that most of the people of the colony were in agreement in their anger at England. Events in the colony soon proved him right. On September 1, 1774, Gage had sent out a small force to capture and destroy a colonial gunpowder supply that was being held in Mystic, now part of Somerville.

What took place next is known as the Powder Alarm. A rumor circulated that the British navy was bombarding Boston and that many people had already died. The next morning, there were 3,000 minutemen assembled in Cambridge, with 10,000 more on the way. As the rumor spread, militia from as far away as the Connecticut River Valley were armed and on their way to Boston. Some believe that as many as 50,000 men were ready to come to Boston's aid.

When the colonials learned that Boston had not been attacked, the start of the war was avoided, at least temporarily. General Gage realized just how small his force was and wrote to England requesting 20,000 troops. He also suggested that the Intolerable Acts be repealed, and that he and his men be allowed to leave Boston and blockade the colony from the sea. While he waited for a response from England, he avoided direct conflict with the colonials and got his men ready for the winter. The boycott of the English was so successful in Massachusetts that Gage could not buy food and other supplies for his soldiers. They were living in tents on Boston Common, and he had to import workers from New York and Nova Scotia to prepare winter quarters for them.

On April 14, 1775, Gage got the answer to his request for more troops from England. Lord William Dartmouth, the British secretary of the colonies, responded on behalf of King George. They felt Gage's request was ridiculous and instructed him to take action. He was to round up the opposition leaders and take whatever steps were necessary to restore British rule to the countryside outside of Boston. Despite his reluctance, Gage was a good soldier and followed his orders.

THE BATTLES OF LEXINGTON AND CONCORD

There were very few secrets in colonial Massachusetts. Although many Loyalists had moved into Boston for their own safety, and many sympathetic to the opposition had moved out for the same reason, there were people reporting everything that went on to both sides. Gage had reports that the leaders of the Sons of Liberty—Sam Adams, John Hancock, and others—were hiding in Lexington and that the minutemen had a store of munitions at Concord. As soon as Gage began to prepare some of his troops for a raid, the colonials knew where they were going. The only thing they did not know was what route the British would take and exactly when they would go.

Paul Revere, William Dawes, and others prepared to watch the routes and raise the alarm as soon as the British left Boston. They

The night of April 18, 1775, Paul Revere completed his midnight ride, during which he warned colonists that the British were heading inland from Boston. *(Library of Congress)*

Paul Revere
(1734–1818)

Paul Revere was one of the top American silversmiths and engravers of his time. He was also a member of Boston's Committee of Correspondence, and he kept people in the outlying towns aware of what General Gage was doing in Boston. He was also a strong supporter of the cause of independence.

During his famous ride that was memorialized inaccurately in the poem "Paul Revere's Ride," by Henry Wadsworth Longfellow, he was captured by a British patrol and held for a short period of time. He is often misquoted as yelling, "The British are coming. The British are coming." The message that was actually called out by Revere and the other riders was, "The regulars are coming out."

A strong supporter of American independence, Paul Revere warned colonists that the British were leaving Boston and preparing to attack. *(From Benson Lossing, The Pictorial Field-book of the Revolution, 1851–1852)*

had agreed to raise one lantern if the British were traveling completely on land. Two lanterns meant the British would cross Back Bay by boat and then march on. When Paul Revere saw the 800 soldiers getting into boats, he sent a messenger to the North Church, and two signal lanterns were hung in the church tower. This told the messengers that the British were traveling by sea, would cross Boston's Back Bay, and then travel out the Concord Road through Lexington. Once the signal was given, the riders sped off into the night, avoiding the British patrols, and sounding the alarm.

By early morning April 19, 1775, the advance column of British troops reached Lexington to find 70 minutemen waiting for them. The colonial leader, Colonel John Parker, realized it would be a foolish waste of lives to fight when outnumbered by so many, and he told his men to run for it. At the same time, the British commander of the advance forces, Major John Pitcairn, ordered the colonials to put down their weapons. When they listened to Parker and tried to leave, the British soldiers started shooting without anyone giving the order to fire. Before Pitcairn could get his men to stop, eight colonists had been killed and 10 others wounded.

Adams and Hancock had already left Lexington, so the British advanced to Concord. There most of the store of weapons had already been moved. Pitcairn had his men burn the few weapons that were left, and they inadvertently set a couple of nearby buildings on fire. The minutemen on their way to Lexington and

The Battles of Lexington and Concord signaled the beginning of the Revolutionary War. *(National Archives, Still Pictures Branch, NWDNS-JKH-JH-3)*

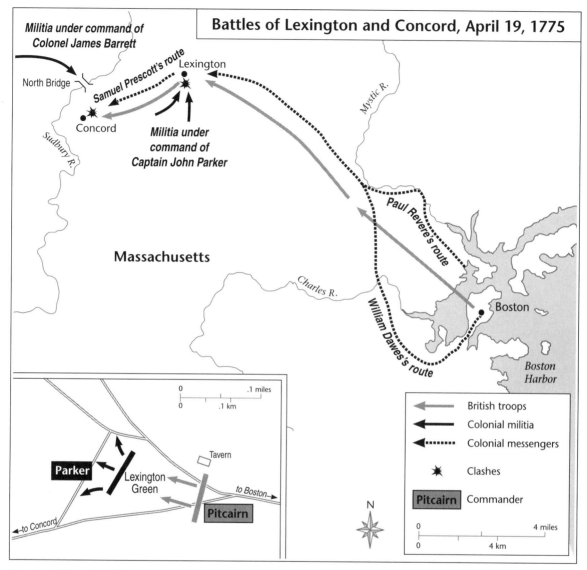

Militia under command of
Colonel James Barrett

North Bridge

Samuel Prescott's route

Lexington

Concord

Militia under
command of
Captain John Parker

Sudbury R.

Mystic R.

Massachusetts

Paul Revere's route

Charles R.

William Dawes's route

Boston

Boston
Harbor

0   .1 miles
0   .1 km

Tavern

Parker

Lexington
Green

to Boston

to Concord

Pitcairn

N

     British troops

     Colonial militia

     Colonial messengers

     Clashes

Pitcairn   Commander

0   4 miles
0   4 km

On the night of April 18, 1775, Paul Revere, William Dawes, and Samuel Prescott sounded the alarm that the British were moving to attack Lexington and Concord. The following day, the first battles of the War for Independence were fought at Lexington and Concord.

Concord saw the smoke and assumed the British were burning the town.

After securing the town, the British sent some soldiers to Colonel James Barrett's farm, where more weapons were supposedly hidden. The weapons at Barrett's had also been moved in expectation of a British search. Barrett watched the British from a hill with a large force of militia. From the hill, Barrett and his men could see the smoke coming from Concord. They decided to attack. When the British reached Concord's North Bridge, Barrett moved his force within 50 yards of the British, and a short skirmish took place. Four of the eight British officers at the bridge were wounded, and their force broke and headed back toward Concord.

The worst trouble for the British came after noon when their commander, Colonel Francis Smith, tried to march his troops back to Boston. By this time, large numbers of armed colonials had rushed to the area. As the British retreated, they constantly came under fire from colonial snipers and engaged in a number of pitched battles. When a relief column of 2,000 British soldiers reached what remained of the 800-man force sent out to Lexington and Concord, 273 British soldiers were dead, wounded, or missing. The colonials lost 95 militia members in the battle, and the War for Independence had begun.

THE BATTLE OF BUNKER HILL

For the next two months, there were no major conflicts between the colonial militias that had gathered around Boston and the British forces that were trapped there. The militia leaders knew they needed to command the high ground around Boston and its harbor if they were going to drive out the British. Plans were made to fortify Dorchester Heights to the south of the city and Breed's and Bunker Hills that overlook the harbor from Charlestown to the north. During the night of June 16, 1775, about 1,000 colonial militiamen went to the top of Breed's and Bunker Hills. It was decided that they would dig in on Breed's Hill, which was not quite as tall as Bunker Hill, but it was closer to the harbor.

When the British soldiers in Boston woke up on June 17, 1775, they were greeted with the sight of the colonial force looking down their rifles at them. The British response was immediate. Warships were brought in to bombard Breed's Hill, and a force of 2,200 redcoats was sent to show the colonials what it was like to face an assault by troops from the greatest army in the world at the time.

General Gage made yet another blunder as he instructed General Howe to lead his forces in a direct frontal assault. The British would learn a very hard lesson on the slopes of Breed's Hill. Instead of panicking in the face of 2,200 British soldiers marching up the hill in formation, Colonel William Prescott had his men hold their fire until the British were almost to them. When the order to fire was given, the colonial marksmen mowed down the British soldiers and sent them retreating down the hill.

Once out of range, the British reset their formations and marched into the colonial sights again. The results were the same: The British suffered even more casualties and were sent back down again. On the third assault, the British finally captured Breed's Hill as the colonials had run out of gunpowder, but British losses were

The Battle of Bunker Hill on June 17, 1775, helped the colonists realize they might have a chance at becoming independent from the British. *(Library of Congress)*

so heavy, they were unable to pursue the American fighters. The records show that 226 British soldiers died and 828 were wounded in capturing Breed's Hill. On the colonial side, 140 were killed and 271 were wounded.

The American Revolution was just starting, and the Battle of Bunker Hill—as it is called, even though it was fought on Breed's Hill—was not a significant victory in terms of territory won and lost. However, in the psychological battle between the mighty British army and the untrained and undisciplined American forces, the impact of the battle on the slopes of Breed's Hill was immense. From this battle forward, the British would proceed with much greater respect for their adversaries and with a sense of caution. Although the colonials lost the hill, they gained a huge boost of confidence. They may not have had fancy red uniforms, but the minutemen of Massachusetts and the surrounding colonies that held in the face of the attacks on Breed's Hill had proved they were a match for the British regulars.

General Gage had now commanded two attacks against the colonial forces. At both Lexington and Concord, and at Breed's Hill, his forces had been shown up by the colonials. When word of the casualties sustained at Breed's Hill reached London, Gage was recalled. General William Howe took over as commander of the British forces in North America. Some have argued that it was Howe's cautious attitude, after leading the attack on Breed's Hill that may have been the key to the American victory in the War for Independence.

THE SECOND CONTINENTAL CONGRESS

Massachusetts sent John Adams, Samuel Adams, and John Hancock as representatives to the Second Continental Congress. This congress convened on May 10, 1775, and stayed in session almost continuously until the new federal constitution went into effect in 1789. One of the first major acts of the congress was the creation of a Continental army and the selection of General George Washington to command it. At this point, the role of the congress changed from a group that was discussing and advising the colonies to one that took charge of a united effort to stop the British.

Governor Hutchinson had told the leaders of Massachusetts that they had to choose between loyalty to the Crown and inde-

The Second Continental Congress convened on May 10, 1775, and remained in session until the newly independent nation had a constitution. *(National Archives, Still Picture Records, NWDNS-148-CCD-35)*

pendence. He, like many other Loyalists, never thought that the majority would pick independence. In London, the feelings were even stronger that they just had to teach the colonists a harsh lesson and that they would then fall back in line. However, on July 4, 1776, the Second Continental Congress made it clear what path they had chosen.

On June 5, 1776, a committee had been appointed by the congress to come up with a declaration regarding the independence of the colonies. John Adams from Massachusetts was appointed to the committee along with Thomas Jefferson, Benjamin Franklin, Roger Sherman, and Robert R. Livingston. Thomas Jefferson is considered to be the person who actually wrote out the committee's document, which would become the Declaration of Indepen-

One of the first and boldest acts of the Second Continental Congress was to compose and sign the Declaration of Independence in the summer of 1776. *(Library of Congress)*

dence on July 4, 1776. When the Continental Congress signed the actual document in August 1776, John Hancock signed first as president of the congress. John Adams, Elbridge Gerry, Samuel Adams, and Robert Treat Paine also signed for Massachusetts.

THE SIEGE OF BOSTON

As the newly appointed commander of the Continental army, George Washington's first task was to drive General Howe out of Boston and liberate the city, which had been occupied since the Intolerable Acts had closed the port in 1774. In winter 1775–76, Washington organized the forces that had assembled around Boston. By March 1776, the city was completely surrounded by the newly formed Continental army as well as numerous militia groups. In the fall, Fort Ticonderoga on Lake Champlain in upstate New York had been captured from the British. The cannons from the fort were placed on sleds and dragged to Boston.

Washington had the cannons set up on Dorchester Heights to the south of Boston. He was prepared to bomb the British positions. General Howe realized that Washington had the advantage and decided he would wait to fight another time. Howe

The First Paragraph of the Declaration of Independence

When in the Course of human events, it becomes necessary for one people to dissolve the political bands which have connected them with another, and to assume among the Powers of the earth, the separate and equal station to which the Laws of Nature and of Nature's God entitle them, a decent respect to the opinions of mankind requires that they should declare the causes which impel them to the separation.

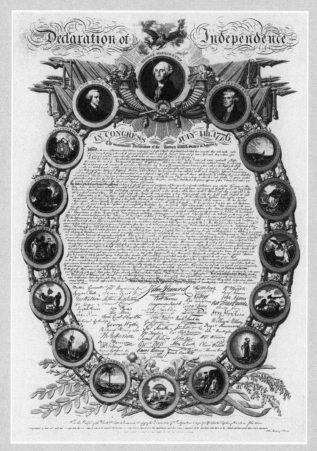

This facsimile of the Declaration of Independence was made in the early 19th century and is surrounded by an ornamental oval frame with medallions of the seals of the 13 original colonies and portraits of John Hancock, George Washington, and Thomas Jefferson. *(Library of Congress, Prints and Photographs Division [LC-USZ62-5780])*

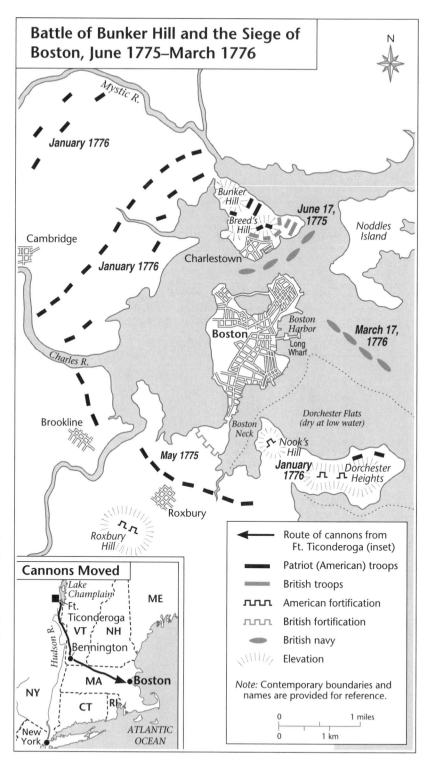

Battle of Bunker Hill and the Siege of Boston, June 1775–March 1776

N

Mystic R.

January 1776

Cambridge

January 1776

Bunker Hill

Breed's Hill

June 17, 1775

Noddles Island

Charlestown

Charles R.

Boston

Boston Harbor

Long Wharf

March 17, 1776

Brookline

Boston Neck

Dorchester Flats (dry at low water)

Nook's Hill

January 1776

Dorchester Heights

May 1775

Roxbury

Roxbury Hill

Cannons Moved

Lake Champlain

Ft. Ticonderoga

ME

Hudson R.

VT

NH

Bennington

MA

Boston

NY

CT

RI

New York

ATLANTIC OCEAN

Route of cannons from Ft. Ticonderoga (inset)

Patriot (American) troops

British troops

American fortification

British fortification

British navy

Elevation

Note: Contemporary boundaries and names are provided for reference.

0   1 miles

0   1 km

After the Battle of Bunker Hill, the colonial forces kept the British pinned down in Boston. The colonials got the edge when cannons captured at Fort Ticonderoga were brought on sleds to Boston. Washington had the cannons set up on Dorchester Heights, where he could fire on the British positions in Boston and British ships in the harbor.

Deborah Sampson
(1760–1827)

At the age of 10, Deborah Sampson became an indentured servant on a farm in Middleborough, Massachusetts. During the eight years of her indenture, she worked alongside the eight sons of the family and learned many skills not usually taught to young girls at the time. She learned to hunt and shoot as well as use most of the tools on the farm. In addition, she learned to read and write, a skill not often shared with young girls in colonial America.

When Sampson had completed her eight-year indenture, she taught school for a while and also traveled from house to house doing spinning and weaving. However, all the talk of the Revolution captured her imagination. On May 20, 1782, she disguised herself as a man and traveled to Worcester, Massachusetts, where she enlisted for a three-year term in the Fourth Massachusetts Regiment of the Continental army.

Using the name Robert Shurtliff, which was the first and middle name of one of her brothers, she went off to war. Supposedly, she was teased by her fellow soldiers for being too young to shave, but she managed to hide her true identity. At one point, she even removed a musket ball from her thigh by herself, rather than take the chance that a doctor would discover she was not a man. She might have served her full term had she not caught a fever during an epidemic that swept Philadelphia in 1783. When nearly unconscious with fever, a doctor examined her and discovered her secret.

After 18 months in the army, Deborah Sampson was given an honorable discharge, on October 25, 1783. When she returned to Massachusetts, she married and had three children. In 1792 she asked the state of Massachusetts for her back wages and was given them. In 1818, Sampson petitioned the U.S. Congress for a veteran's pension and received that as well.

abandoned Boston to Washington and his forces on March 17, 1776. Many Loyalists left with Howe. Some went to Nova Scotia, while others went to England.

The Siege of Boston was the end of the war fought in Massachusetts. However, soldiers from Massachusetts were a part of the Continental army throughout the war. The records show that units from Massachusetts followed Washington from Boston until the end of the fighting at Yorktown, Virginia, in 1783.

9

Creating the State of Massachusetts

A STATE CONSTITUTION

As soon as independence was declared in 1776, many states began the task of creating state constitutions. In Massachusetts,

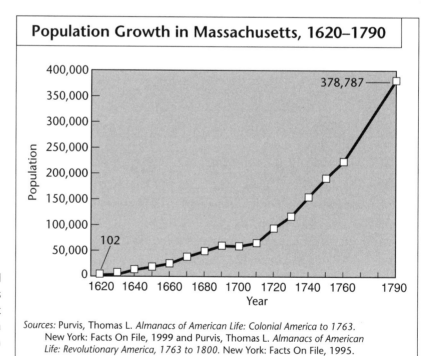

Population Growth in Massachusetts, 1620–1790

378,787

Sources: Purvis, Thomas L. *Almanacs of American Life: Colonial America to 1763.* New York: Facts On File, 1999 and Purvis, Thomas L. *Almanacs of American Life: Revolutionary America, 1763 to 1800.* New York: Facts On File, 1995.

Throughout the colonial period, Massachusetts was the second most populated colony. Virginia was the only colony with more people.

John Hancock
(1737–1793)

As president of the Second Continental Congress when the Declaration of Independence was signed, John Hancock was given the honor of being the first to sign. It has since become one of the most recognized signatures in the U.S. history. In fact, the phrase "put your John Hancock on it" has become part of the American language and means putting one's signature on a document.

Hancock grew up in Braintree, Massachusetts, as a friend of John Adams. When he was orphaned, he was adopted by his uncle, Thomas Hancock, who was one of the wealthiest men in the colony. Thomas sent his nephew to Boston Latin School and then on to Harvard, and eventually left him his business and fortune.

John Hancock became embroiled in the Patriot cause when the sloop he owned, *Liberty*, was seized by the customs authorities for smuggling in a load of wine without paying taxes. The seizure of the boat on June 10, 1768, set off riots in Boston, and when the sloop was condemned by the court and put into service by the customs agent, another mob took to the streets and burned the Liberty.

Hancock's vigorous defense of the Liberty in court, even though he lost the case, brought him to the attention of the Patriot leaders, whom he joined. It was Hancock and Samuel Adams who the British were trying to arrest in April 1775, when they attacked Lexington and Concord. When the British offered a general pardon after the battle to participants who would lay down their guns and take an oath of allegiance to the Crown, Hancock and Sam Adams were specifically excluded from the offer.

Hancock was so popular in Massachusetts that he was elected governor nine times between 1780 and his death in 1793.

people proceeded with more caution. When the provisional legislature called for a constitutional convention in 1776, it was defeated. Feeling a need for a constitution, the legislature drew up one on its own in 1778, and it failed to be ratified by the voters. In spring 1779, the towns finally voted to hold a state constitutional convention that would have broad participation from all the towns.

Part of the reluctance to create a formal state government in Massachusetts was the problem of trying to satisfy the varying interests and factions within the state. Massachusetts was divided in a number of ways. In the eastern part of the state, there was a striking division between the wealthy merchants and business

John Adams
(1735–1826)

John Adams was one of Massachusetts's most talented leaders during the struggle for independence and in the early years of the new republic. As a lawyer in Boston, he had been involved in the Patriot cause almost from the beginning. Not even his defense of the soldiers who fired into the crowd during the Boston Massacre dampened his popularity. Prior to the Declaration of Independence, Adams served in the First Continental Congress, as well as being active in Massachusetts.

Adams wrote a number of articles and pamphlets in support of actions against the British and for independence. Although Thomas Jefferson is credited with being the principal author of the Declaration of Independence, Adams served on the committee that brought the document before the Second Continental Congress. He and Benjamin Franklin are credited with suggesting changes to Jefferson's early drafts. Adams was also the spokesperson for the committee and convinced many reluctant delegates to vote in favor of declaring independence.

Adams was also farsighted enough to know that all the colonies had to be involved if the War for Independence was to succeed. Adams had this in mind when he pushed for George Washington to head the Continental army instead of his fellow delegate and lifelong friend from Massachusetts, John Hancock, who had lobbied for the job. Adams wanted to be sure that Virginia, which was where Washington was from, and was the only colony with more

people and the lower classes. There was also a strong division between the eastern and western halves of the state. The economy of the west was completely dependent upon agriculture, while the east looked to the sea for commerce.

When the state constitutional convention finally convened in September 1779, there was much wrangling over how people would be represented and who would be allowed to hold office and vote. Eventually, it fell to John Adams to try and create a document that would serve the Commonwealth and satisfy the various factions.

The constitution that Adams drafted for Massachusetts called for a government with a strong governor, an upper and lower house in the legislature, and an independent judiciary. The new state constitution was adopted in 1780, and John Hancock was elected as the first governor.

people than Massachusetts, would fully support the war.

During the war, Adams represented the united colonies overseas. He spent several years in France, and in 1783, Adams, along with Benjamin Franklin and John Jay, negotiated the Treaty of Paris with Britain, bringing the War of Independence to an end. He then served as the Continental Congress's representative to Britain from 1785–88.

It is believed that James Madison, one of the principal authors of the U.S. Constitution, used Adams's Massachusetts constitution as a model. When the new constitution went into effect, Adams came in second in the electoral voting for the country's first president. He served as George Washington's vice president for eight years and then served one term as the country's second president.

John Adams served in both Continental Congresses and was instrumental in the creation of the Declaration of Independence. *(Library of Congress)*

It was during the governorship of James Bowdoin (1785–89) that the new state of Massachusetts and the struggling new nation had its most serious test.

SHAYS'S REBELLION

Although the troubles that pitted western Massachusetts against the eastern establishment in 1786 and 1787 are referred to as Shays's Rebellion, the problem was much greater than can be defined by one man. Daniel Shays, like many of the farmers in Massachusetts at the time, was caught in a spiraling trap of debt. After the war ended, prices had fallen sharply for farm produce, and many farmers found themselves in a financial crisis. Some ended up in jail because of their inability to pay their debts. Many others were in court, trying to keep their farms while holding off their creditors.

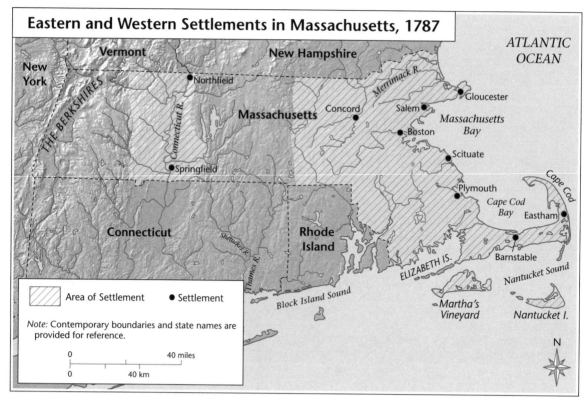

Eastern and Western Settlements in Massachusetts, 1787

The members of the Massachusetts Bay Colony spread out from Cape Ann to lands along the Charles and Mystic Rivers in what are today the cities of Charlestown, Boston, Cambridge, Watertown, and so on.

To make matters worse, Governor Bowdoin was leading the state down a rough path, as he tried to raise taxes to pay off the debt the state had accumulated during the war. The new taxes were to be collected in specie (coin), something the western farmers had very few of. The farmers also knew that the state had borrowed heavily from the wealthy Patriot merchants of Boston and the other Massachusetts ports. Many of these men had profited greatly from the war. They had been paid well by the states and Continental Congress for shipping the goods that were needed to keep the Continental army fighting. Many also profited greatly by outfitting some of their ships as privateers, capturing valuable cargos that were meant for the British troops in North America. Many farmers thought they were the victims of a conspiracy by the wealthy merchants and politicians in the eastern half of the state.

PENNSYLVANIA, ſſ.

By the *Prefident* and the *Supreme Ex*ecutive *Council* of the Commonwealth of *Pennſylvania,*

A PROCLAMATION.

WHEREAS the General Aſſembly of this Commonwealth, by a law entituled 'An act for co-operating with " the ſtate of Maſſachuſetts bay, agreeable to the articles of " confederation, in the apprehending of the proclaimed rebels " DANIEL SHAYS, LUKE DAY, ADAM WHEELER " and ELI PARSONS," have enacted, " that rewards ad- " ditional to thoſe offered and promiſed to be paid by the ſtate " of Maſſachuſetts Bay, for the apprehending the aforeſaid " rebels, be offered by this ſtate ;" WE do hereby offer the following rewards to any perſon or perſons who ſhall, within the limits of this ſtate, apprehend the rebels aforeſaid, and ſecure them in the gaol of the city and county of Philadelphia, ⸻ viz. For the apprehending of the ſaid Daniel Shays, and ſecuring him as aforeſaid, the reward of *One hundred and Fifty Pounds* lawful money of the ſtate of Maſſachuſetts Bay, and *One Hundred Pounds* lawful money of this ſtate ; and for the apprehending the ſaid Luke Day, Adam Wheeler and Eli Parſons, and ſecuring them as aforeſaid, the reward (reſpectively) of *One Hundred Pounds* lawful money of Maſſachuſetts Bay and *Fifty Pounds* lawful money of this ſtate : And all judges, juſtices, ſheriffs and conſtables are hereby ſtrictly enjoined and required to make diligent ſearch and enquiry after, and to uſe their utmoſt endeavours to apprehend and ſecure the ſaid Daniel Shays, Luke Day, Adam Wheeler and Eli Parſons, their aiders, abettors and comforters, and every of them, ſo that they may be dealt with according to law.

GIVEN in Council, under the hand of the Preſident, and the Seal of the State, at Philadelphia, this tenth day of March, in the year of our Lord one thouſand ſeven hundred and eighty-ſeven.

BENJAMIN FRANKLIN.

ATTEST
JOHN ARMSTRONG, jun. Secretary.

This proclamation by the state of Pennsylvania offers a reward for Daniel Shays and three other people who participated in Shays's Rebellion, which included a march on the Massachusetts armory in Springfield.
(Library of Congress, Prints and Photographs Division [LC-USZ62-77992])

Many farmers who joined Daniel Shays were veterans of the Revolutionary War and felt that the current situation was not what they had fought for. Having organized and succeeded in overthrowing the British, it must have seemed like the only way to solve the problem with the other half of Massachusetts was in the same way. The farmers held town meetings during summer and fall 1786, condemning the government in Boston and closing the courts that were putting their neighbors in jail.

That winter, on January 25, 1787, 2,000 angry and armed farmers marched on the Massachusetts armory at Springfield. The state had sent militia general William Shepard and 600 men to protect the armory. When Shepard ordered the farmers to turn around and go home, they continued toward the armory. Shepard had some of his men fire warning shots, which also failed to stop the seasoned combat veterans. At this point, General Shepard had only two choices: give up the armory or fire on the farmers.

General Shepard had his men fire their cannon into the farmers. Four men were killed and 20 or more were wounded. The farmers quickly dispersed. It was one thing to organize a protest, but it was another thing to charge into cannon fire. After the encounter at Springfield Armory, the state sent more militia from the east under the command of General Benjamin Lincoln. They fought a number of skirmishes with the farmers before Shays and some of the other leaders fled to Rhode Island and then north to Vermont.

Massachusetts was not the only state where there was a serious problem of debtors. The economic depression that came with the end of the war reached into every corner of the United States during 1786 and 1787. Courts were forced by angry mobs to close in Rhode Island, South Carolina, and Maryland. The farmers of

As governor of New York, George Clinton helped develop a strong government in that colony. Because Clinton feared that Shays's Rebellion would grow, he ordered that rebellion participants be arrested if discovered in New York. *(Library of Congress, Prints and Photographs Division [LC-USZ62-74112])*

New Hampshire surrounded the state legislature demanding relief from the problem. George Clinton, governor of New York, was so worried about Shays's Rebellion spilling over the border into New York that he ordered the arrest of any participants of the Massachusetts rebellion who entered New York.

As soon as the Massachusetts militia regained control of the western part of the state, leniency was shown to the participants in the rebellion. All the farmers who had been involved in the rebellion, except Shays and three other leaders, were immediately granted pardons for the treasonous attacks on the state. Shays and his coleaders were tried for treason, convicted, and then they too were pardoned.

Shays's Rebellion did not really threaten the stability of the new United States, but it did show that the Articles of Confederation had a number of flaws. First, under the Articles, the national government had no authority to assist in the suppression of Shays's Rebellion. Probably even more important was the fact that the government in Philadelphia was ineffective in dealing with the nation's economic problems. In Massachusetts, the next round of elections brought a legislative majority to those who wanted to help the farmers of western Massachusetts with their economic crisis. Nationally, the rebellion played an important role in shaping the new federal constitution.

10

Building a Strong Nation

At the beginning of 1787, the call went out to all 13 state legislatures to send delegates to a convention in Philadelphia in May to suggest revisions to the Articles of Confederation. The Articles of Confederation had been proposed in 1777 and finally adopted by all the states in 1781. They had seen the states through to the successful completion of the war, but in peacetime a number of shortcomings had become apparent. The Articles made no provisions for the national government to deal with trade and numerous problems that had arisen between the states. And Shays's Rebellion had pointed out the inability of the national government to deal with the economy and civil unrest.

Twelve states sent a total of 55 delegates to Philadelphia. Rhode Island never participated in the framing of the constitution. Although the delegates were there to revise the Articles of Confederation, they almost immediately began to write a new constitution. Under the rules of the convention, each state had a minimum of four representatives. On matters before the convention, each state would have one vote. The representatives of only seven of the states needed to be present for the convention to conduct business and only a simple majority of the states present was needed to pass something.

Massachusetts sent four delegates to Pennsylvania: Elbridge Gerry, Nathaniel Gorham, Rufus King, and Caleb Strong. All four

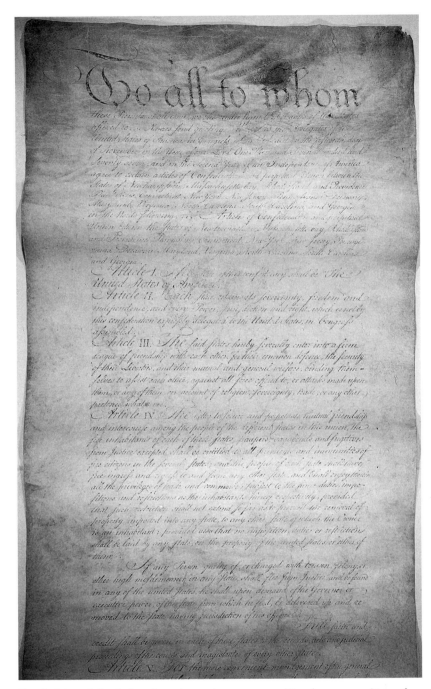

The Articles of Confederation, shown here, were written by a committee of the Continental Congress and intended as a constitution for the colonies.
(National Archives, National Archives Building, NWCTB-360-MISC-ROLL10F81)

Caleb Strong served as a Massachusetts delegate to the Constitutional Convention and would later be governor of the state. *(Library of Congress, Prints and Photographs Division [LC-USZ62-93490])*

were accomplished in local, state, and national politics and, with the exception of Gorham, would continue in public service most of their lives. Gerry and Strong would both be governors of the state in the future. Gerry served as James Madison's vice president and died in 1814 on his way to preside over the Senate. King later moved to New York and unsuccessfully ran for president in 1816.

In the end, three of the four Massachusetts delegates supported the new constitution and worked to have it ratified in Massachusetts. Only Gerry, among the Massachusetts delegation, refused to sign the constitution at the end of the convention. Caleb Strong did not sign either, but that was because he was called home early because of an illness in his family.

Massachusetts convened a state convention to discuss and vote on the proposed U.S. Constitution in the early days of 1788. By that time, five states had already voted to ratify, and nine were needed to set up the new federal government. Many believe that had the new Constitution been put to a popular vote in all 13 states, it would not have been ratified. By holding state conventions, debate took place, and the Federalists, those in favor of the Constitution, could work to convince those who opposed it.

As the Massachusetts convention began, it looked like a majority of the delegates were opposed. Many still remembered the days of colonial tyranny, and feared that a strong central government would not be responsive to the needs and liberties of individuals. Eventually, the Massachusetts convention was swayed by two of Massachusetts's most famous Patriots: Samuel Adams and John Hancock. On February 6, 1788, the Massachusetts convention voted 187 to 168 in favor of the Constitution, and the state became the sixth to ratify it.

Elbridge Gerry
(1744–1814)

Elbridge Gerry was born in 1744 into one of Marblehead, Massachusetts's wealthiest merchant families. After graduating from Harvard in 1762, he went to work in his father's business. They were a part of the cod trade and shipped dried and salted cod to the Caribbean and Europe, and exchanged it for sugar in the islands and wine and manufactured goods in Europe. When Boston harbor was closed by the Intolerable Acts in 1774, Gerry and other merchants in Marblehead brought in many of the goods

Elbridge Gerry, a Massachusetts delegate to the Constitutional Convention, helped frame the U.S. Constitution. Gerry later served as governor of Massachusetts. *(Library of Congress, Prints and Photographs Division [LC-USZ62-111790])*

that were sent from the other colonies to help the people of Boston.

He was deeply involved in the politics of independence. He served with Samuel Adams and John Hancock on the council of safety, and he was almost arrested with them on the eve of the Battles of Lexington and Concord. Gerry went on to serve in the Continental Congress, where he distinguished himself with his knowledge of commerce and finance. At the Constitutional Convention, he was one of the most active delegates.

When the Convention reached an impasse between the Virginia Plan that favored the large states and the New Jersey Plan that helped the smaller states, Gerry was made chairman of the committee that produced what has become known as the Great Compromise. The compromise created the current U.S. federal legislative bodies, where the House of Representatives is proportional based on population and the Senate has two senators from each state no matter the state's size.

Despite his active participation in the framing of the Constitution, Gerry refused to sign it because of two primary concerns. First, unlike Adams's state constitution, the federal constitution did not include a bill of rights. His other objection was he thought the Constitution did not do enough to ensure the rights of the individual states. When it came time to ratify the Constitution

(continues)

(continued)

in Massachusetts, Gerry was a vocal opponent to ratification.

In 1789, Gerry finally added his support to the new federal government and was elected to the first Congress. In the ensuing years, he served two terms as governor of Massachusetts and would end his political career as James Madison's vice president. During his term as governor, he was responsible for redistricting the state. He and his political allies created oddly shaped districts so they would have electoral majorities. They created one district that ended up looking like a salamander on the map. To ridicule Gerry, his opponents referred to the oddly shaped district as a "gerrymander," a term that is still used in political discussion about redistricting today.

With the aid of Samuel Adams, John Hancock helped convince the Massachusetts convention to ratify the Constitution. Hancock's signature is the most prominent on that earlier revolutionary document—the Declaration of Independence. *(National Archives, Still Picture Records, NWDNS-148-CD-4[23])*

It took until June 21, 1788, for New Hampshire to become the ninth state to ratify the Constitution and set the wheels turning to reorganize the federal government. It was May 1790, before the 13th state, Rhode Island, finally ratified the Constitution in their legislature, by a vote of 34 to 32.

By the time of ratification, the economy of Massachusetts had recovered from the postwar depression, and even the farmers of the western part of the state were experiencing the prosperity of the strengthened United States. Bradford, Winthrop, and the other early Puritan leaders would have found the United States near the end of the 18th century hard to believe. Yet in part, it was their desire to have the freedom to worship as they saw fit and to create a place where their ideals could be followed that led to the creation of the United States.

Preamble to the U.S. Constitution

We the People of the United States, in Order to form a more perfect Union, establish Justice, insure domestic Tranquility, provide for the common defence, promote the general Welfare, and secure the Blessings of Liberty to ourselves and our Posterity, do ordain and establish this Constitution for the United States of America.

Massachusetts Time Line

1602

★ Gosnold explores the Massachusetts coast.

1614

★ John Smith maps the Massachusetts coast.

1620

★ Pilgrims land at Plymouth.

1628

★ Salem is founded.

1629

★ The Massachusetts Bay Company is started.

1630

★ Dorchester becomes the capital of the Massachusetts Bay Colony.

1632

★ Boston becomes the capital of the Massachusetts Bay Colony.

1636
★ Harvard College is founded.

1643
★ Puritans form the New England Confederation.

1660
★ The Stuarts are restored to the throne in England.

1675–77
★ King Philip's War is fought.

1685
★ Massachusetts loses charter and becomes part of the Dominion of New England under Sir Edmund Andros.

1689
★ Andros is arrested in Boston. The Dominion of New England dissolves.

1689–97
★ King William's War is fought.

1691
★ Massachusetts becomes a royal province with a governor appointed by the king of England. The province retains Maine and its two legislative houses.

1692
★ Witchcraft trials are held in Boston.

1702–13
★ Queen Anne's War is fought.

1704
★ Deerfield is attacked.

1744–48

★ King George's War is fought.

1745

★ Massachusetts forms part of the force that defeats the French at Louisbourg on Cape Breton (it was later returned to the French).

1764

★ The Sugar Act is passed.

1765

★ The Stamp Act is passed.

1766

★ Protests against the Sugar Act bring about its repeal.

1770

★ In an event that will become known as the Boston Massacre, British troops in Boston fire into a crowd.

1773

★ The Tea Act is passed; Boston residents retaliate by dumping tea into Boston harbor, an action that becomes known as the "Boston Tea Party."
★ The Continental Congress convenes and orders a boycott of British goods.

1775

★ The Siege of Boston occurs.
★ **April 19:** Paul Revere and William Dawes ride out to warn colonists of the coming of British troops. The Battles of Lexington and Concord are fought.
★ **June:** The Battle of Bunker Hill is fought.

1776

★ **March 17:** The British evacuate Massachusetts.

1786–87

★ Shays's Rebellion occurs.

1788

★ **February 6:** Massachusetts becomes the sixth state to ratify the U.S. Constitution.

Massachusetts Historical Sites

BOSTON

Boston Common   Located in downtown Boston, it is where cattle grazed and it served as a training ground for the military. It was bought from William Blaxton in 1634 for $150. It was used by the British as a mustering ground before the Battle of Bunker Hill.

> *Address:* Boston Common Visitor Information Center,
>   147 Tremont Street, Boston, MA 02116
> *Phone:* 617-536-4100
> *Web Site:* www.mass-vacation.com

Bunker Hill National Historic Landmark   The British stormed Breed's Hill in Charlestown on June 17, 1775, after the Battles of Lexington and Concord. An obelisk 221 feet high commemorates the battle.

> *Address:* Bunker Hill Lodge, Monument Square, Charlestown,
>   MA 02129
> *Phone:* 617-242-5641
> *Web Site:* www.nps.gov/bost/index/htm

Dorchester Heights National Historic Site   Cannons seized by Ethan Allen at Fort Ticonderoga were moved to Dorchester

Heights, arriving in March 1776. Patriots under George Washington fired heavily on the British from Dorchester Heights, causing the British to end their occupation of Boston on March 17, 1776.

Address: Thomas Park, South Boston, MA 02127
Phone: 617-242-5642

Freedom Trail   This 90-minute, 2.5-mile walking tour led by National Park Service Rangers is free and runs from April through November. Tours start at the Downtown Visitor Center.

Address: 15 State Street, Boston, MA 02109
Phone: 617-242-5642
Web Site: www.nps.gov/bost/freedom_trail.htm

Old North Church   Built in 1723 by William Price, it is the oldest church building in Boston. It was where signal lanterns were hung to let patriots know the British troops were en route to Lexington and Concord.

Address: 193 Salem Street, Boston, MA 02113
Phone: 617-523-4848
Web Site: www.oldnorth.com

Old South Meetinghouse National Historic Landmark   Many protests against the British were held at Old South Meetinghouse. The signal for the Boston Tea Party was given there. British General Burgoyne used it as a riding school for his troops.

Address: 310 Washington Street, Boston, MA 02108
Phone: 617-482-6439
Web Site: www.oldsouthmeetinghouse.org

Paul Revere House National Historic Landmark   Built around 1670, it is the oldest frame house in Boston. Paul Revere bought it in 1770 and his famous ride started from there.

Address: 19 North Street, Boston, MA 02113
Phone: 617-523-2338
Web Site: www.paulreverehouse.org

CONCORD

Minute Man National Historical Park   This park includes over 900 acres with such features as the North Bridge Visitor Center and part of the April 19, 1775, battle road.

   Address: 174 Liberty Street, Concord, MA 01742
   Phone: 978-369-6993
   Web Site: www.nos.gov/mima

DEERFIELD

Old Deerfield Village National Historic Landmark   Founded in 1665, this town was the site of the Bloody Brook Massacre in 1675 and the Great Deerfield Massacre in 1704, when half the town burned.

   Address: The Street (off Routes 5 and 10), Deerfield, MA
     01342
   Phone: 413-774-5581
   Web Site: www.historic-deerfield.org

LEXINGTON

Buckman Tavern National Historic Landmark   The minutemen met at this tavern on the morning of April 19, 1775, before the battle.

   Address: 1 Bedford Street, Lexington, MA 02420
   Phone: 781-862-5598, 781-862-1703
   Web Site: www.lexingtonhistory.org

Hancock-Clarke House National Historic Landmark   John Hancock and Samuel Adams were staying there April 18, 1775, the night before the battle.

   Address: 36 Hancock Street. Lexington, MA 02420
   Phone: 781-862-1703
   Web Site: www.lexingtonhistory.org

Lexington Green National Historic Landmark Lexington Green is the site of the Battle of Lexington, where minutemen met British soldiers under Lieutenant Colonel Francis Smith.

> *Address:* Lexington Visitor Center, 1875 Massachusetts Avenue, Lexington, MA 02421
> *Phone:* 781-862-1450

PLYMOUTH

Cole's Hill National Historic Landmark Many of the people who died the first year after landing in Plymouth in December 1620 were buried here. There is also a statue of Massasoit.

> *Address:* Carver Street, Plymouth, MA 02360

Mayflower II This ship is a full-size copy of the original that brought the Pilgrims to America.

> *Address:* State Pier, Plymouth, MA 02360
> *Phone:* 508-746-1622
> *Web Site:* www.plimoth.org

Plimoth Plantation This museum recreates life in Plymouth in 1627.

> *Address:* Route 3, Exit 4, 137 Warren Avenue, Plymouth, MA 02360
> *Mailing Address:* Box 1620, Plymouth, MA 02362
> *Phone:* 508-746-1622
> *Web Site:* www.plimoth.org

Plymouth Rock The Pilgrims landed at this site.

> *Address:* Water Street, Plymouth, MA 02360
> *Web Site:* www.plymouth.org

QUINCY

Adams National Historic Site John and Abigail Adams raised their family here. Later it was the summer home of their son, John Quincy Adams.

Address: 135 Adams Street, Quincy, MA 02169
Phone: 617-770-1175
Web Site: www.nps.gov/adam

SALEM

Salem Maritime National Historic Site   This site includes Derby Wharf, Derby House, West India Goods Store, Scale House, and Bonded Warehouse.

Address: 174 Derby Street, Salem, MA 01970
Phone: 978-740-1650, 978-740-1660
Web Site: www.nps.gov/sama

The Witch House   This house was the home of Jonathan Corwin, one of the judges during the witch trials. It was built in 1642.

Address: 310 $^1/_2$ Essex Street, Salem, MA 01970
Phone: 978-744-0180
Web Site: www.salemweb.com/witchhouse/default.htm

SUDBURY

Longfellow's Wayside Inn State Historic Landmark   Built between 1686 and 1702 by Samuel Howe, it is thought to be the oldest working inn in the United States.

Address: Boston Post Road (off Route 20), Sudbury, MA
    01776
Phone: 978-443-1776, 800-339-1776
Web Site: www.wayside.org

STURBRIDGE

Old Sturbridge Village   This educational museum recreates 18th-century life in a farming town, with 40 buildings open to the public, including a working gristmill.

Address: 1 Old Sturbridge Village Road, Sturbridge, MA 01566
Phone: 508-347-3362
Web Site: www.osv.org

Further Reading

BOOKS

Bjornlund, Lydia. *Massachusetts.* San Diego: Lucent, 2002.

Brown, Richard D., and Jack Tager. *Massachusetts, a Concise History.* Amherst, Mass.: University of Massachusetts Press, 2000.

Connelly, Ellen Russell. *John Winthrop.* Broomall, Pa.: Chelsea House, 2001.

Fradin, Dennis B. *The Massachusetts Colony.* Chicago: Children's Press, 1987.

Kallen, Stuart A. *The Salem Witch Trials.* San Diego: Lucent, 1999.

Lutz, Norma Jean. *Cotton Mather.* Broomall, Pa.: Chelsea House, 2000.

WEB SITES

Boston Online. "Boston links—History." Available online. URL: www.boston-online.com/History/index.html. Downloaded on July 9, 2003.

Cline, Duane. "The Pilgrims and Plymouth Colony, 1620." Available online. URL: www.rootsweb.com/~mosmd/index.htm. Updated on March, 2003.

"Citizen Information Service. Massachusetts Facts. Part Two." Available online. URL: http://www.state.ma.us/sec/cis/cismaf/mf2.htm. Downloaded on August 17, 2003.

Deetz, Patricia Scott, and Christopher Fennell. "The Plymouth Colony Archive Project at the University of Virginia." Available online. URL: etext.lib.virginia.edu/users/deetz. Updated on May 5, 2003.

"Interactive State House." Available online. URL: www.state.ma. us/statehouse/history.htm. Downloaded on July 9, 2003.

Media 3, Inc. "America's Homepage Plymouth, Massachusetts." Available online. URL: pilgrims.net/plymouth. Downloaded on July 9, 2003.

National Geographic Society. "Salem Witchcraft Hysteria." Available online. URL: www.nationalgeographic.com/features/97/ Salem. Downloaded on July 9, 2003.

University of Oklahoma Law Center. "The 1629 Charter of Massachusetts Bay." Available online. URL: www.law.ou.edu/hist/ massbay.html. Downloaded on July 9, 2003.

Index

Page numbers in *italic* indicate photographs. Page numbers in **boldface** indicate box features. Page numbers followed by m indicate maps. Page numbers followed by c indicate time line entries. Page numbers followed by t indicate a table or graph.

and Intolerable Acts 94
Paul Revere and **99**
communion 69
Concord, Battle of. *See* Lexington and Concord, Battle of
Concord, Massachusetts 131
Connecticut xivm
  and Battle of Louisbourg 72
  land issues with 38
  Native Americans in 33–37
Connecticut River Valley
  forts in 70
  and independence movement 96–97
  in King Philip's War 38, 39
  in Queen Anne's War 63, 64
  settlement of 33
Constitution. *See* U.S. Constitution
constitution, state 110–113
Constitutional Convention 118, 120, **121**
Continental army
  creation of 104
  Deborah Sampson and **109**
  siege of Boston 106, 109
Continental Congress, First
  John Adams and **112**
  convening of 95, 127c
  and Suffolk Resolves **94,** 95
Continental Congress, Second 105, 106
  John Adams and **112**
  Articles of Confederation 119
  convening of 104–106
  Elbridge Gerry and **121**
  John Hancock and **111**
  privateers used by **68**
  Thanksgiving day declared by **19**
corn 2, 16, 17
Cotton, John **31, 60**
Court of Oyer and Terminer 58
courts 80–82, 113, 116
covenant of faith **31**
covenant of work **31**
Crispus Attucks Monument **89**

Cromwell, Oliver 45, 45–46
  and Charles II **49**
  and James II **51**
customs agents
  and Boston Massacre 86
  John Hancock and **111**
  and Sugar Act 80, 82
Customs House (Boston) 87, 88

D

Danvers, Massachusetts **63**
Dark Ages ix
Dartmouth, Lord William 97
Dartmouth (ship) 93
Dawes, William 97, 101m, 127c
Daye, Stephen **48**
debt
  of farmers 113, 114
  from King William's War 55
  from Seven Years' War 77
  from War of Independence 114
decapitation 35, 42
Declaration of Independence 106, 107
  John Adams and **112**
  Samuel Adams and **85**
  first paragraph of **107**
  John Hancock and **111,** 122
  writing of the 105–106
Declaratory Act (1766) 86
Deerfield, Massachusetts 64, 64, 126c, 131
defense of colonies 77, 81, 82
Delaware xivm
Dermer, Thomas **14**
A Description of New England (John Smith) 1
dice, stamps required on 82
diplomacy **113**
disease
  and Battle of Louisbourg 74
  in Massachusetts Bay Colony 23
  and Native Americans 5, 9, **14, 15,** 16, **36**
  and witchcraft **59**
dissent 29, 30, 32
distilleries 66, 80

diversity 69
Dominion of New England 52m, 126c
  end of 53, **61**
  establishment of 50
  James II and **51**
  Cotton Mather and **61**
Dorchester, Massachusetts 125c
Dorchester Company 20, 22
Dorchester Heights 102, 106, 108m
Dorchester Heights National Historic Site 129–130
dried cod **26, 121**
drought **19**
drunkenness 66
Dudley, John 65
Dudley, Joseph 66
Dudley, Thomas **25**
Duke of York 51
Dutch
  colonization by xi–xii
  trade with 92
Dutch East India Company xiii
duty taxes 86. *See also* taxation/taxes

E

Eastern Woodland Indians 1
East Florida xivm
East India Company 92
economic independence 25
economy 116, 117, 122
education 26–27, **28**
Edwards, Jonathan 69
Eleanor (ship) 93
Endecott, John 34
England xi
  colonization by xii
  Squanto in **14**
English Civil War 44–47, 45
  Charles II and **49**
  James II and **51**
English language **14**
engravers **99**
Europe, changes in ix–x
evacuation of British 109, 128c
Exeter, New Hampshire **31**

U.S. Constitution
  John Adams and **113**
  Samuel Adams and **85**
  Articles of Confederation as 119
  Preamble to the **123**
  ratification of xivm, **19,** 120,
    122, 128c
  and Shays's Rebellion 117
U.S. House of Representatives **121**
U.S. Senate **121**
Utrecht, Peace of (treaty) 66

V

Vane, Henry **31**
venison **19**
veterans 116
veteran's pension **109**
Vice Admiralty Court 82
Vikings ix, x
villages, Native American 4, 4–5
Virginia
  John Adams and **112–113**
  and Pilgrims 6
  population in colonial 110
  in Seven Years' War 74
  slavery in **89**
  John Smith's map of 2
  U.S. Constitution ratified by xivm
Virginia Plan **121**
visible church **22**
Vodun **59**
Voodoo **59**
voting rights 28

W

Wales 69
Walker, Robert 45
Wampanoag Indians 2
  at first Thanksgiving 18, **19**
  in King Philip's War 38, 38–39

and Plymouth Colony 9, 15, 16,
  18
Squanto **14–15,** 15, 16
wampum 4, 4
Wamsutta 39
War of Austrian Succession. *See* King
  George's War
War of Independence. *See* American
  Revolution
War of the League of Augsburg. *See*
  King William's War
War of the Spanish Succession. *See*
  Queen Anne's War
Warren, Joseph **94**
Warren, Peter 71
Washington, George
  John Adams and **112–113**
  and Continental Congress 104
  and siege of Boston 106, 109
  thanksgiving day declared by
    19
Watertown, Massachusetts 22
West Africans **59**
Western Niantic Indians 34
West Florida xivm
Wethersfield, Connecticut 33, 34
wheat 17
Wheelright, John **31**
Whigs 89, 92
White, Peregrine 12
William and Mary **53,** 54
William Henry, Fort 75
William III (king of Great Britain)
  60. *See also* William and Mary
Williams, Abigail **63**
Williams, John 64
Williams, Roger
  and Anne Marbury Hutchinson
    31
  and Native Americans **36,** 39

and Puritan beliefs **23**
and Puritans 30, 32
Wilson, Josiah 39
Windsor, Connecticut 33
wine **121**
Winslow, Josiah 39, 41
winter
  of 1620–1621 12, 14
  of 1621–1622 17–18
  of 1630–1631 22, 23
Winthrop, John
  and Anne Dudley Bradstreet **25**
  Charles I and 44
  and charter of colony 25, 28
  and cod **26**
  and Anne Marbury Hutchinson
    31
  Massachusetts Bay Colony led by
    21, 22
  and Puritan beliefs **23**
  and Roger Williams 32
witchcraft **59**
  the Mathers and **61**
  the Parris family and **63**
  trials 55–62, 58, 126c
The Witch House 133
witch hunts **23**
women
  at Harvard **28**
  and religious dissent **31**
Wonders of the Invisible World (Cotton
  Mather) **61**
wood 23
Woodbridge, John **25**
Worcester, England **49**
work **31**

Y

Yale College 69
Yorktown, Virginia 109